Contents

THE PELICAN SHAKESPEARE
GENERAL EDITORS

STEPHEN ORGEL
A. R. BRAUNMULLER

The Second Part of
King Henry the Fourth

William Macready as Henry IV, c. 1830

William Shakespeare

The Second Part of
King Henry the Fourth

EDITED BY CLAIRE MCEACHERN

PENGUIN BOOKS

PENGUIN BOOKS

Published by the Penguin Group

Penguin Group (USA) Inc., 375 Hudson Street, New York, New York 10014, U.S.A.

Penguin Group (Canada), 90 Eglinton Avenue East, Suite 700, Toronto,
Ontario, Canada M4P 2Y3 (a division of Pearson Penguin Canada Inc.)

Penguin Books Ltd, 80 Strand, London WC2R 0RL, England

Penguin Ireland, 25 St Stephen's Green, Dublin 2, Ireland (a division of Penguin Books Ltd)

Penguin Group (Australia), 250 Camberwell Road, Camberwell,
Victoria 3124, Australia (a division of Pearson Australia Group Pty Ltd)

Penguin Books India Pvt Ltd, 11 Community Centre, Panchsheel Park, New Delhi – 110 017, India

Penguin Group (NZ), cnr Airborne and Rosedale Roads,
Albany, Auckland 1310, New Zealand (a division of Pearson New Zealand Ltd)

Penguin Books (South Africa) (Pty) Ltd, 24 Sturdee Avenue,
Rosebank, Johannesburg 2196, South Africa

Penguin Books Ltd, Registered Offices: 80 Strand, London WC2R 0RL, England

The Second Part of King Henry the Fourth edited by
Allan G. Chester published in the United States of America
in Penguin Books 1957
Revised edition published 1970
This new edition edited by Claire McEachern published 2000

10   12   14   16   17   15   13   11

ISBN 978-0-14-071457-9

Printed in the United States of America
Set in Garamond
Designed by Virginia Norey

Publisher's Note

IT IS ALMOST half a century since the first volumes of the Pelican Shakespeare appeared under the general editorship of Alfred Harbage. The fact that a new edition, rather than simply a revision, has been undertaken reflects the profound changes textual and critical studies of Shakespeare have undergone in the past twenty years. For the new Pelican series, the texts of the plays and poems have been thoroughly revised in accordance with recent scholarship, and in some cases have been entirely reedited. New introductions and notes have been provided in all the volumes. But the new Shakespeare is also designed as a successor to the original series; the previous editions have been taken into account, and the advice of the previous editors has been solicited where it was feasible to do so.

Certain textual features of the new Pelican Shakespeare should be particularly noted. All lines are numbered that contain a word, phrase, or allusion explained in the glossarial notes. In addition, for convenience, every tenth line is also numbered, in italics when no annotation is indicated. The intrusive and often inaccurate place headings inserted by early editors are omitted (as is becoming standard practice), but for the convenience of those who miss them, an indication of locale now appears as the first item in the annotation of each scene.

In the interest of both elegance and utility, each speech prefix is set in a separate line when the speaker's lines are in verse, except when those words form the second half of a verse line. Thus the verse form of the speech is kept visually intact. What is printed as verse and what is printed as prose has, in general, the authority of the original texts. Departures from the original texts in this regard have only the authority of editorial tradition and the judgment of the Pelican editors; and, in a few instances, are admittedly arbitrary.

The Theatrical World

ECONOMIC REALITIES determined the theatrical world in which Shakespeare's plays were written, performed, and received. For centuries in England, the primary theatrical tradition was nonprofessional. Craft guilds (or "mysteries") provided religious drama – mystery plays – as part of the celebration of religious and civic festivals, and schools and universities staged classical and neoclassical drama in both Latin and English as part of their curricula. In these forms, drama was established and socially acceptable. Professional theater, in contrast, existed on the margins of society. The acting companies were itinerant; playhouses could be any available space – the great halls of the aristocracy, town squares, civic halls, inn yards, fair booths, or open fields – and income was sporadic, dependent on the passing of the hat or on the bounty of local patrons. The actors, moreover, were considered little better than vagabonds, constantly in danger of arrest or expulsion.

In the late 1560s and 1570s, however, English professional theater began to gain respectability. Wealthy aristocrats fond of drama – the Lord Admiral, for example, or the Lord Chamberlain – took acting companies under their protection so that the players technically became members of their households and were no longer subject to arrest as homeless or masterless men. Permanent theaters were first built at this time as well, allowing the companies to control and charge for entry to their performances.

Shakespeare's livelihood, and the stunning artistic explosion in which he participated, depended on pragmatic and architectural effort. Professional theater requires ways to restrict access to its offerings; if it does not, and admission fees cannot be charged, the actors do not get paid, the costumes go to a pawnbroker, and there is no such thing as a professional, ongoing theatrical tradition. The answer to that economic need arrived in the late 1560s and 1570s with the creation of the so-called public or amphitheater playhouse. Recent discoveries indicate that the precursor of the Globe playhouse in London (where Shakespeare's mature plays were presented) and the Rose theater (which presented Christopher Marlowe's plays and some of Shakespeare's earliest ones) was the Red Lion theater of 1567. Archaeological studies of the foundations of the Rose and Globe theaters have revealed that the open-air theater of the 1590s and later was probably a polygonal building with fourteen to twenty or twenty-four sides, multistoried, from 75 to 100 feet in diameter, with a raised, partly covered "thrust" stage that projected into a group of standing patrons, or "groundlings," and a covered gallery, seating up to 2,500 or more (very crowded) spectators.

These theaters might have been about half full on any given day, though the audiences were larger on holidays or when a play was advertised, as old and new were, through printed playbills posted around London. The metropolitan area's late-Tudor, early-Stuart population (circa 1590-1620) has been estimated at about 150,000 to 250,000. It has been supposed that in the mid-1590s there were about 15,000 spectators per week at the public theaters; thus, as many as 10 percent of the local population went to the theater regularly. Consequently, the theaters' repertories – the plays available for this experienced and frequent audience – had to change often: in the month between September 15 and October 15, 1595, for instance, the Lord Admiral's Men performed twenty-eight times in eighteen different plays.

Since natural light illuminated the amphitheaters' stages, performances began between noon and two o'clock and ran without a break for two or three hours. They often concluded with a jig, a fencing display, or some other nondramatic exhibition. Weather conditions determined the season for the amphitheaters: plays were performed every day (including Sundays, sometimes, to clerical dismay) except during Lent – the forty days before Easter – or periods of plague, or sometimes during the summer months when law courts were not in session and the most affluent members of the audience were not in London.

To a modern theatergoer, an amphitheater stage like that of the Rose or Globe would appear an unfamiliar mixture of plainness and elaborate decoration. Much of the structure was carved or painted, sometimes to imitate marble; elsewhere, as under the canopy projecting over the stage, to represent the stars and the zodiac. Appropriate painted canvas pictures (of Jerusalem, for example, if the play was set in that city) were apparently hung on the wall behind the acting area, and tragedies were accompanied by black hangings, presumably something like crepe festoons or bunting. Although these theaters did not employ what we would call scenery, early modern spectators saw numerous large props, such as the "bar" at which a prisoner stood during a trial, the "mossy bank" where lovers reclined, an arbor for amorous conversation, a chariot, gallows, tables, trees, beds, thrones, writing desks, and so forth. Audiences might learn a scene's location from a sign (reading "Athens," for example) carried across the stage (as in Bertolt Brecht's twentieth-century productions). Equally captivating (and equally irritating to the theater's enemies) were the rich costumes and personal props the actors used: the most valuable items in the surviving theatrical inventories are the swords, gowns, robes, crowns, and other items worn or carried by the performers.

Magic appealed to Shakespeare's audiences as much as it does to us today, and the theater exploited many deceptive and spectacular devices. A winch in the loft above the stage, called "the heavens," could lower and raise actors playing gods, goddesses, and other supernatural figures to and from the main acting area, just as one or more trapdoors permitted entrances and exits to and from the area, called "hell," beneath the stage. Actors wore elementary makeup such as wigs, false beards, and face paint, and they employed pig's bladders filled with animal blood to make wounds seem more real. They had rudimentary but effective ways of pretending to behead or hang a person. Supernumeraries (stagehands or actors not needed in a particular scene) could make thunder sounds (by shaking a metal sheet or rolling an iron ball down a chute) and show lightning (by blowing inflammable resin through tubes into a flame). Elaborate fireworks enhanced the effects of dragons flying through the air or imitated such celestial phenomena as comets, shooting stars, and multiple suns. Horses' hoofbeats, bells (located perhaps in the tower above the stage), trumpets and drums, clocks, cannon shots and gunshots, and the like were common sound effects. And the music of viols, cornets, oboes, and recorders was a regular feature of theatrical performances.

For two relatively brief spans, from the late 1570s to 1590 and from 1599 to 1614, the amphitheaters competed with the so-called private, or indoor, theaters, which originated as, or later represented themselves as, educational institutions training boys as singers for church services and court performances. These indoor theaters had two features that were distinct from the amphitheaters': their personnel and their playing spaces. The amphitheaters' adult companies included both adult men, who played the male roles, and boys, who played the female roles; the private, or indoor, theater companies, on the other hand, were entirely composed of boys aged about 8 to 16, who were, or could pretend to be, candidates for singers in a church or a royal boys' choir. (Until 1660, professional theatrical companies included no women.) The playing space would appear much more familiar to modern audiences than the long-vanished amphitheaters; the later indoor theaters were, in fact, the ancestors of the typical modern theater. They were enclosed spaces, usually rectangular, with the stage filling one end of the rectangle and the audience arrayed in seats or benches across (and sometimes lining) the building's longer axis. These spaces staged plays less frequently than the public theaters (perhaps only once a week) and held far fewer spectators than the amphitheaters: about 200 to 600, as opposed to 2,500 or more. Fewer patrons mean a smaller gross income, unless each pays more. Not surprisingly, then, private theaters charged higher prices than the amphitheaters, probably sixpence, as opposed to a penny for the cheapest entry.

Protected from the weather, the indoor theaters presented plays later in the day than the amphitheaters, and used artificial illumination – candles in sconces or candelabra. But candles melt, and need replacing, snuffing, and trimming, and these practical requirements may have been part of the reason the indoor theaters introduced breaks in the performance, the intermission so dear to the heart of theatergoers and to the pocketbooks of theater concessionaires ever since. Whether motivated by the need to tend to the candles or by the entrepreneurs' wishing to sell oranges and liquor, or both, the indoor theaters eventually established the modern convention of the non-continuous performance. In the early modern "private" theater, musical performances apparently filled the intermissions, which in Stuart theater jargon seem to have been called "acts."

At the end of the first decade of the seventeenth century, the distinction between public amphitheaters and private indoor companies ceased. For various cultural, political, and economic reasons, individual companies gained control of both the public, open-air theaters and the indoor ones, and companies mixing adult men and boys took over the formerly "private" theaters. Despite the death of the boys' companies and of their highly innovative theaters (for which such luminous playwrights as Ben Jonson, George Chapman, and John Marston wrote), their playing spaces and conventions had an immense impact on subsequent plays: not merely for the intervals (which stressed the artistic and architectonic importance of "acts"), but also because they introduced political and social satire as a popular dramatic ingredient, even in tragedy, and a wider range of actorly effects, encouraged by their more intimate playing spaces.

Even the briefest sketch of the Shakespearean theatrical world would be incomplete without some comment on the social and cultural dimensions of theaters and playing in the period. In an intensely hierarchical and status-conscious society, professional actors and their ventures had hardly any respectability; as we have indicated, to protect themselves against laws designed to curb vagabondage and the increase of masterless men, actors resorted to the near-fiction that they were the servants of noble masters, and wore their distinctive livery. Hence the company for which Shakespeare wrote in the 1590s called itself the Lord Chamberlain's Men and pretended that the public, money-getting performances were in fact rehearsals for private performances before that high court official. From 1598, the Privy Council had licensed theatrical companies, and after 1603, with the accession of King James I, the companies gained explicit royal protection, just as the Queen's Men had for a time under Queen Elizabeth. The Chamberlain's Men became the King's Men, and the other companies were patronized by the other members of the royal family.

These designations were legal fictions that half-concealed an important economic and social development, the evolution away from the theater's organization on the model of the guild, a self-regulating confraternity of individual artisans, into a proto-capitalist organization. Shakespeare's company became a joint-stock company, where persons who supplied capital and, in some cases, such as Shakespeare's, capital and talent, employed themselves and others in earning a return on that capital. This development meant that actors and theater companies were outside both the traditional guild structures, which required some form of civic or royal charter, and the feudal household organization of master-and-servant. This anomalous, maverick social and economic condition made theater companies practically unruly and potentially even dangerous; consequently, numerous official bodies – including the London metropolitan and ecclesiastical authorities as well as, occasionally, the royal court itself – tried, without much success, to control and even to disband them.

Public officials had good reason to want to close the theaters: they were attractive nuisances – they drew often riotous crowds, they were always noisy, and they could be politically offensive and socially insubordinate. Until the Civil War, however, anti-theatrical forces failed to shut down professional theater, for many reasons – limited surveillance and few police powers, tensions or outright hostilities among the agencies that sought to check or channel theatrical activity, and lack of clear policies for control. Another reason must have been the theaters' undeniable popularity. Curtailing any activity enjoyed by such a substantial percentage of the population was difficult, as various Roman emperors attempting to limit circuses had learned, and the Tudor-Stuart audience was not merely large, it was socially diverse and included women. The prevalence of public entertainment in this period has been underestimated. In fact, fairs, holidays, games, sporting events, the equivalent of modern parades, freak shows, and street exhibitions all abounded, but the theater was the most widely and frequently available entertainment to which people of every class had access. That fact helps account both for its quantity and for the fear and anger it aroused.

WILLIAM SHAKESPEARE OF
STRATFORD-UPON-AVON, GENTLEMAN

Many people have said that we know very little about William Shakespeare's life – pinheads and postcards are often mentioned as appropriately tiny surfaces on which to record the available information. More imaginatively and perhaps more correctly, Ralph Waldo Emerson wrote, "Shakespeare is the only biographer of Shakespeare. . . . So far from Shakespeare's being the least known, he is the one person in all modern history fully known to us."

In fact, we know more about Shakespeare's life than we do about almost any other English writer's of his era. His last will and testament (dated March 25, 1616) survives, as do numerous legal contracts and court documents involving Shakespeare as principal or witness, and parish records in Stratford and London. Shakespeare appears quite often in official records of King James's royal court, and of course Shakespeare's name appears on numerous title pages and in the written and recorded words of his literary contemporaries Robert Greene, Henry Chettle, Francis Meres, John Davies of Hereford, Ben Jonson, and many others. Indeed, if we make due allowance for the bloating of modern, run-of-the-mill bureaucratic records, more information has survived over the past four hundred years about William Shakespeare of Stratford-upon-Avon, Warwickshire, than is likely to survive in the next four hundred years about any reader of these words.

What we do not have are entire categories of information – Shakespeare's private letters or diaries, drafts and revisions of poems and plays, critical prefaces or essays, commendatory verse for other writers' works, or instructions guiding his fellow actors in their performances, for instance – that we imagine would help us understand and appreciate his surviving writings. For all we know, many such data never existed as written records. Many literary and theatrical critics, not knowing what might once have existed, more or less cheerfully accept the situation; some even make a theoretical virtue of it by claiming that such data are irrelevant to understanding and interpreting the plays and poems.

So, what do we know about William Shakespeare, the man responsible for thirty-seven or perhaps more plays, more than 150 sonnets, two lengthy narrative poems, and some shorter poems?

While many families by the name of Shakespeare (or some variant spelling) can be identified in the English Midlands as far back as the twelfth century, it seems likely that the dramatist's grandfather, Richard, moved to Snitterfield, a town not far from Stratford-upon-Avon, sometime before 1529. In Snitterfield, Richard Shakespeare leased farmland from the very wealthy Robert Arden. By 1552, Richard's son John had moved to a large house on Henley Street in Stratford-upon-Avon, the house that stands today as "The Birthplace." In Stratford, John Shakespeare traded as a glover, dealt in wool, and lent money at interest; he also served in a variety of civic posts, including "High Bailiff," the municipality's equivalent of mayor. In 1557, he married Robert Arden's youngest daughter, Mary. Mary and John had four sons – William was the oldest – and four daughters, of whom only Joan outlived her most celebrated sibling. William was baptized (an event entered in the Stratford parish church records) on April 26, 1564, and it has become customary, without any good factual support, to suppose he was born on April 23, which happens to be the feast day of Saint George, patron saint of England, and is also the date on which he died, in 1616. Shakespeare married Anne Hathaway in 1582, when he was eighteen and she was twenty-six; their first child was born five months later. It has been generally assumed that the marriage was enforced and subsequently unhappy, but these are only assumptions; it has been estimated, for instance, that up to one third of Elizabethan brides were pregnant when they married. Anne and William Shakespeare had three children: Susanna, who married a prominent local physician, John Hall; and the twins Hamnet, who died young in 1596, and Judith, who married Thomas Quiney – apparently a rather shady individual. The name Hamnet was unusual but not unique: he and his twin sister were named for their godparents, Shakespeare's neighbors Hamnet and Judith Sadler. Shakespeare's father died in 1601 (the year of *Hamlet*), and Mary Arden Shakespeare died in 1608 (the year of *Coriolanus*). William Shakespeare's last surviving direct descendant was his granddaughter Elizabeth Hall, who died in 1670.

Between the birth of the twins in 1585 and a clear reference to Shakespeare as a practicing London dramatist in Robert Greene's sensationalizing, satiric pamphlet, *Greene's Groatsworth of Wit* (1592), there is no record of where William Shakespeare was or what he was doing. These seven so-called lost years have been imaginatively filled by scholars and other students of Shakespeare: some think he traveled to Italy, or fought in the Low Countries, or studied law or medicine, or worked as an apprentice actor/writer, and so on to even more fanciful possibilities. Whatever the biographical facts for those "lost" years, Greene's nasty remarks in 1592 testify to professional envy and to the fact that Shakespeare already had a successful career in London. Speaking to his fellow playwrights, Greene warns both generally and specifically:

> . . . trust them [actors] not: for there is an upstart crow, beautified with our feathers, that with his tiger's heart wrapped in a player's hide supposes he is as well able to bombast out a blank verse as the best of you; and being an absolute Johannes Factotum, is in his own conceit the only Shake-scene in a country.

The passage mimics a line from *3 Henry VI* (hence the play must have been performed before Greene wrote) and seems to say that "Shake-scene" is both actor and playwright, a jack-of-all-trades. That same year, Henry Chettle protested Greene's remarks in *Kind-Heart's Dream,* and each of the next two years saw the publication of poems – *Venus and Adonis* and *The Rape of Lucrece,* respectively – publicly ascribed to (and dedicated by) Shakespeare. Early in 1595 he was named one of the senior members of a prominent acting company, the Lord Chamberlain's Men, when they received payment for court performances during the 1594 Christmas season.

Clearly, Shakespeare had achieved both success and reputation in London. In 1596, upon Shakespeare's application, the College of Arms granted his father the now-familiar coat of arms he had taken the first steps to obtain almost twenty years before, and in 1598, John's son – now permitted to call himself "gentleman" – took a 10 percent share in the new Globe playhouse. In 1597, he bought a substantial bourgeois house, called New Place, in Stratford – the garden remains, but Shakespeare's house, several times rebuilt, was torn down in 1759 – and over the next few years Shakespeare spent large sums buying land and making other investments in the town and its environs. Though he worked in London, his family remained in Stratford, and he seems always to have considered Stratford the home he would eventually return to. Something approaching a disinterested appreciation of Shakespeare's popular and professional status appears in Francis Meres's *Palladis Tamia* (1598), a not especially imaginative and perhaps therefore persuasive record of literary reputations. Reviewing contemporary English writers, Meres lists the titles of many of Shakespeare's plays, including one not now known, *Love's Labor's Won,* and praises his "mellifluous & hony-tongued" "sugred Sonnets," which were then circulating in manuscript (they were first collected in 1609). Meres describes Shakespeare as "one of the best" English playwrights of both comedy and tragedy. In *Remains . . . Concerning Britain* (1605),

William Camden – a more authoritative source than the imitative Meres – calls Shakespeare one of the "most pregnant witts of these our times" and joins him with such writers as Chapman, Daniel, Jonson, Marston, and Spenser. During the first decades of the seventeenth century, publishers began to attribute numerous play quartos, including some non-Shakespearean ones, to Shakespeare, either by name or initials, and we may assume that they deemed Shakespeare's name and supposed authorship, true or false, commercially attractive.

For the next ten years or so, various records show Shakespeare's dual career as playwright and man of the theater in London, and as an important local figure in Stratford. In 1608-9 his acting company – designated the "King's Men" soon after King James had succeeded Queen Elizabeth in 1603 – rented, refurbished, and opened a small interior playing space, the Blackfriars theater, in London, and Shakespeare was once again listed as a substantial sharer in the group of proprietors of the playhouse. By May 11, 1612, however, he describes himself as a Stratford resident in a London lawsuit – an indication that he had withdrawn from day-to-day professional activity and returned to the town where he had always had his main financial interests. When Shakespeare bought a substantial residential building in London, the Blackfriars Gatehouse, close to the theater of the same name, on March 10, 1613, he is recorded as William Shakespeare "of Stratford upon Avon in the county of Warwick, gentleman," and he named several London residents as the building's trustees. Still, he continued to participate in theatrical activity: when the new Earl of Rutland needed an allegorical design to bear as a shield, or *impresa,* at the celebration of King James's Accession Day, March 24, 1613, the earl's accountant recorded a payment of 44 shillings to Shakespeare for the device with its motto.

For the last few years of his life, Shakespeare evidently

concentrated his activities in the town of his birth. Most of the final records concern business transactions in Stratford, ending with the notation of his death on April 23, 1616, and burial in Holy Trinity Church, Stratford-upon-Avon.

THE QUESTION OF AUTHORSHIP

The history of ascribing Shakespeare's plays (the poems do not come up so often) to someone else began, as it continues, peculiarly. The earliest published claim that someone else wrote Shakespeare's plays appeared in an 1856 article by Delia Bacon in the American journal *Putnam's Monthly* – although an Englishman, Thomas Wilmot, had shared his doubts in private (even secretive) conversations with friends near the end of the eighteenth century. Bacon's was a sad personal history that ended in madness and poverty, but the year after her article, she published, with great difficulty and the bemused assistance of Nathaniel Hawthorne (then United States Consul in Liverpool, England), her *Philosophy of the Plays of Shakspere Unfolded*. This huge, ornately written, confusing farrago is almost unreadable; sometimes its intents, to say nothing of its arguments, disappear entirely beneath near-raving, ecstatic writing. Tumbled in with much supposed "philosophy" appear the claims that Francis Bacon (from whom Delia Bacon eventually claimed descent), Walter Ralegh, and several other contemporaries of Shakespeare's had written the plays. The book had little impact except as a ridiculed curiosity.

Once proposed, however, the issue gained momentum among people whose conviction was the greater in proportion to their ignorance of sixteenth- and seventeenth-century English literature, history, and society. Another American amateur, Catherine P. Ashmead Windle, made the next influential contribution to the cause when she published *Report to the British Museum* (1882), wherein she promised to open "the Cipher of Francis Bacon," though what she mostly offers, in the words of S. Schoenbaum, is "demented allegorizing." An entire new cottage industry grew from Windle's suggestion that the texts contain hidden, cryptographically discoverable ciphers – "clues" – to their authorship; and today there are not only books devoted to the putative ciphers, but also pamphlets, journals, and newsletters.

Although Baconians have led the pack of those seeking a substitute Shakespeare, in *"Shakespeare" Identified* (1920), J. Thomas Looney became the first published "Oxfordian" when he proposed Edward de Vere, seventeenth earl of Oxford, as the secret author of Shakespeare's plays. Also for Oxford and his "authorship" there are today dedicated societies, articles, journals, and books. Less popular candidates – Queen Elizabeth and Christopher Marlowe among them – have had adherents, but the movement seems to have divided into two main contending factions, Baconian and Oxfordian. (For further details on all the candidates for "Shakespeare," see S. Schoenbaum, *Shakespeare's Lives,* 2nd ed., 1991.)

The Baconians, the Oxfordians, and supporters of other candidates have one trait in common – they are snobs. Every pro-Bacon or pro-Oxford tract sooner or later claims that the historical William Shakespeare of Stratford-upon-Avon could not have written the plays because he could not have had the training, the university education, the experience, and indeed the imagination or background their author supposedly possessed. Only a learned genius like Bacon or an aristocrat like Oxford could have written such fine plays. (As it happens, lucky male children of the middle class had access to better education than most aristocrats in Elizabethan England – and Oxford was not particularly well educated.) Shakespeare received in the Stratford grammar school a formal education that would daunt many college graduates today; and popular rival playwrights such as the very learned Ben Jonson and George Chapman, both of whom also lacked university training, achieved great artistic success, without being taken as Bacon or Oxford.

Besides snobbery, one other quality characterizes the authorship controversy: lack of evidence. A great deal of testimony from Shakespeare's time shows that Shakespeare wrote Shakespeare's plays and that his contemporaries recognized them as distinctive and distinctly superior. (Some of that contemporary evidence is collected in E. K. Chambers, *William Shakespeare: A Study of Facts and Problems*, 2 vols., 1930.) Since that testimony comes from Shakespeare's enemies and theatrical competitors as well as from his co-workers and from the Elizabethan equivalent of literary journalists, it seems unlikely that, if any one of these sources had known he was a fraud, they would have failed to record that fact.

Books About Shakespeare's Theater

Useful scholarly studies of theatrical life in Shakespeare's day include: G. E. Bentley, *The Jacobean and Caroline Stage*, 7 vols. (1941–68), and the same author's *The Professions of Dramatist and Player in Shakespeare's Time, 1590–1642* (1986); E. K. Chambers, *The Elizabethan Stage*, 4 vols. (1923); R. A. Foakes, *Illustrations of the English Stage, 1580–1642* (1985); Andrew Gurr, *The Shakespearean Stage*, 3rd ed. (1992), and the same author's *Play-going in Shakespeare's London*, 2nd ed. (1996); Edwin Nungezer, *A Dictionary of Actors* (1929); Carol Chillington Rutter, ed., *Documents of the Rose Playhouse* (1984).

Books About Shakespeare's Life

The following books provide scholarly, documented accounts of Shakespeare's life: G. E. Bentley, *Shakespeare: A Biographical Handbook* (1961); E. K. Chambers, *William Shakespeare: A Study of Facts and Problems*, 2 vols. (1930); S. Schoenbaum, *William Shakespeare: A Compact*

Documentary Life (1977); and *Shakespeare's Lives,* 2nd ed. (1991), by the same author. Many scholarly editions of Shakespeare's complete works print brief compilations of essential dates and events. References to Shakespeare's works up to 1700 are collected in C. M. Ingleby et al., *The Shakespeare Allusion-Book,* rev. ed., 2 vols. (1932).

The Texts of Shakespeare

As far as we know, only one manuscript conceivably in Shakespeare's own hand may (and even this is much disputed) exist: a few pages of a play called *Sir Thomas More*, which apparently was never performed. What we do have, as later readers, performers, scholars, students, are printed texts. The earliest of these survive in two forms: quartos and folios. Quartos (from the Latin for "four") are small books, printed on sheets of paper that were then folded in fours, to make eight double-sided pages. When these were bound together, the result was a squarish, eminently portable volume that sold for the relatively small sum of sixpence (translating in modern terms to about $5.00). In folios, on the other hand, the sheets are folded only once, in half, producing large, impressive volumes taller than they are wide. This was the format for important works of philosophy, science, theology, and literature (the major precedent for a folio Shakespeare was Ben Jonson's *Works*, 1616). The decision to print the works of a popular playwright in folio is an indication of how far up on the social scale the theatrical profession had come during Shakespeare's lifetime. The Shakespeare folio was an expensive book, selling for between fifteen and eighteen shillings, depending on the binding (in modern terms, from about $150 to $180). Twenty Shakespeare plays of the thirty-seven that survive first appeared in quarto, seventeen of which appeared during Shakespeare's lifetime; the rest of the plays are found only in folio.

The First Folio was published in 1623, seven years after Shakespeare's death, and was authorized by his fellow actors, the co-owners of the King's Men. This publication was certainly a mark of the company's enormous respect for Shakespeare; but it was also a way of turning the old plays, most of which were no longer current in the playhouse, into ready money (the folio includes only Shakespeare's plays, not his sonnets or other nondramatic verse). Whatever the motives behind the publication of the folio, the texts it preserves constitute the basis for almost all later editions of the playwright's works. The texts, however, differ from those of the earlier quartos, sometimes in minor respects but often significantly – most strikingly in the two texts of *King Lear*, but also in important ways in *Hamlet, Othello,* and *Troilus and Cressida.* (The variants are recorded in the textual notes to each play in the new Pelican series.) The differences in these texts represent, in a sense, the essence of theater: the texts of plays were initially not intended for publication. They were scripts, designed for the actors to perform – the principal life of the play at this period was in performance. And it follows that in Shakespeare's theater the playwright typically had no say either in how his play was performed or in the disposition of his text – he was an employee of the company. The authoritative figures in the theatrical enterprise were the shareholders in the company, who were for the most part the major actors. They decided what plays were to be done; they hired the playwright and often gave him an outline of the play they wanted him to write. Often, too, the play was a collaboration: the company would retain a group of writers, and parcel out the scenes among them. The resulting script was then the property of the company, and the actors would revise it as they saw fit during the course of putting it on stage. The resulting text belonged to the company. The playwright had no rights in it once he had been paid. (This system survives largely intact in the movie industry, and most of the playwrights of Shakespeare's time were as anonymous as most screenwriters are today.) The script could also, of course, continue to change as the tastes of audiences and the requirements of the actors changed. Many – perhaps most – plays were revised when they were reintroduced after any substantial absence from the repertory, or when they were performed by a company different from the one that originally commissioned the play.

Shakespeare was an exceptional figure in this world because he was not only a shareholder and actor in his company, but also its leading playwright – he was literally his own boss. He had, moreover, little interest in the publication of his plays, and even those that appeared during his lifetime with the authorization of the company show no signs of any editorial concern on the part of the author. Theater was, for Shakespeare, a fluid and supremely responsive medium – the very opposite of the great classic canonical text that has embodied his works since 1623.

The very fluidity of the original texts, however, has meant that Shakespeare has always had to be edited. Here is an example of how problematic the editorial project inevitably is, a passage from the most famous speech in *Romeo and Juliet*, Juliet's balcony soliloquy beginning "O Romeo, Romeo, wherefore art thou Romeo?" Since the eighteenth century, the standard modern text has read,

> What's Montague? It is nor hand, nor foot,
> Nor arm, nor face, nor any other part
> Belonging to a man. O be some other name!
> What's in a name? That which we call a rose
> By any other name would smell as sweet.
>
> (II.2.40-44)

Editors have three early texts of this play to work from, two quarto texts and the folio. Here is how the First Quarto (1597) reads:

> Whats *Mountague?* It is nor band nor foote,
> Nor arme, nor face, nor any other part.
> Whats in a name? That which we call a Rose,
> By any other name would smell as sweet:

Here is the Second Quarto (1599):

> Whats *Mountague?* it is nor hand nor foote,
> Nor arme nor face, ô be some other name
> Belonging to a man.
> Whats in a name that which we call a rose,
> By any other word would smell as sweete,

And here is the First Folio (1623):

> What's *Mountague?* it is nor hand nor foote,
> Nor arme, nor face, O be some other name
> Belonging to a man.
> What? in a names that which we call a Rose,
> By any other word would smell as sweete,

There is in fact no early text that reads as our modern text does – and this is the most famous speech in the play. Instead, we have three quite different texts, all of which are clearly some version of the same speech, but none of which seems to us a final or satisfactory version. The transcendently beautiful passage in modern editions is an editorial invention: editors have succeeded in conflating and revising the three versions into something we recognize as great poetry. Is this what Shakespeare "really" wrote? Who can say? What we can say is that Shakespeare always had performance, not a book, in mind.

Books About the Shakespeare Texts

The standard study of the printing history of the First Folio is W. W. Greg, *The Shakespeare First Folio* (1955). J. K. Walton, *The Quarto Copy for the First Folio of Shakespeare* (1971), is a useful survey of the relation of the quartos to the folio. The second edition of Charlton Hinman's *Norton Facsimile* of the First Folio (1996), with a new introduction by Peter Blayney, is indispensable. Stanley Wells and Gary Taylor, *William Shakespeare: A Textual Companion,* keyed to the Oxford text, gives a comprehensive survey of the editorial situation for all the plays and poems.

THE GENERAL EDITORS

Introduction

LONG BEFORE HOLLYWOOD, Shakespeare was a master of the art of the sequel. In *2 Henry IV* he returns to his own popular story line and renders it both familiar and afresh. But because this is Shakespeare, in the process of satisfying our desire to revisit the past he causes us to examine our own appetite for such a return – and, ultimately, painfully, to renounce it.

2 Henry IV is the third play in what is termed the Henriad, the four-history-play sequence that reaches from *Richard II* to *Henry V* and takes for its primary narrative material the political events that broached the Wars of the Roses during the fifteenth century. *2 Henry IV* was entered in the Stationers' Register in August 1600; however, the play is thought to have been written before the end of 1598, close on the heels of *1 Henry IV* (c. 1596-97), whose characters and plotline it resumes. The deposition of King Richard II by Henry Bolingbroke (Henry IV) and the ensuing civil chaos provide the matter for much of this "second tetralogy" (so named because it follows, compositionally, the suite of four plays concerning the latter part of the Wars of the Roses). The turmoil of civil war shares space with and provides a context for the tale of a ruler's coming-of-age.

A short-lived but successful king, as far as victory in foreign war was concerned, Henry V was renowned in Shakespeare's Elizabethan England primarily for two things: his underdog victory over the king of France at the battle of Agincourt, and his prodigal youth. By the time Shakespeare directed his attention to him, he was the subject of legend, that of a miraculous conversion from a profligate prince to a Christian king. The first part of

Henry IV introduces Prince Hal amid his tavern companions, his royal father's worst nightmare; in the course of the play we witness him reveling with the best of them in the tavern (Falstaff not least of these), but also as he answers the call to battle at Shrewsbury, where he nobly distinguishes himself by saving the king from danger and slaying the leader of the rebel faction, Henry Percy of Northumberland (Hotspur). At the end of this play he stands poised between the bodies of the dissolute knight Falstaff and the brave warrior Hotspur, a tableau that seems to represent the dual forces that pull upon Prince Hal. Falstaff, however, is only playing dead, and bounds up to claim credit for the death of Hotspur, a credit Hal allows him to claim despite his knowledge that it is a bogus one. We leave this play with the rebel forces defeated, Hal and Falstaff together again, and a general sense of order, at least temporarily, restored.

2 Henry IV, however, reveals the provisional quality of this resolution. The play picks up where its predecessor leaves off, with the wake of Shrewsbury and yet more civil war, and superficially follows the scheme of the previous play in much of its pacing and events: the alternation of scenes of warriors and revelers; the preparations for a battle; the face-off between royal and rebel forces on the battlefield; and the resolution, where Hal stands before us in a newly achieved identity, reunited with Falstaff. Yet as if to prove the point that you can't, even in a history play, go home again, Shakespeare's return to this world renders it both the same and irrevocably changed, a deliberate and distorted echo of its former self.

This is an exhausted world, one shuddering in civil unrest. Old, ill, and dying men dominate the play: an aged and broken Northumberland, deluded in his hopes of a rebel victory and cruelly bereft of his seemingly indomitable son Hotspur by his own failure to support him at Shrewsbury; Falstaff, gout-ridden, preoccupied with his doctor's opinion of his urine and with his dwindling funds; Justice Shallow, doddering in his reminiscences of youth and fumbling in his covetousness for the future; Henry IV, too ill to savor the news of his son John's "victory" over the rebels at Gaultree Forest; and the Lord Chief Justice, fearful for his future under his former nemesis, Prince Henry, and wishing that his time on earth, like the king's, was finished: "I would his majesty had called me with him." Falstaff and the Lord Chief Justice argue over who is the least elderly; the embarrassing effect is of seeing two geezers beat each other with their canes.

This is a country of old men, and if the fathers of this universe are fast slouching toward their end, the world they have left behind them is the worse for wear as well. Even rebellion seems to lack its former energy, and the causes that claimed the passions and lives of such as Hotspur no longer command the same zeal. Archbishop Scroop tries to reanimate his insurrection with the same terms as before, and "doth enlarge his rising with the blood / Of fair King Richard," but they lack luster and seem merely a cynical cover for what is, more baldly, revenge for the previous defeat. There is a sense of aging quarrels trying to feed themselves by any means; old duels, old decrees, and old causes hover like ghosts over these wars, although it becomes harder and harder to remember their origins or to invest them with their former meaning.

The battle itself is anticlimactic, indeed nonexistent. The thrilling confusion, the risk-taking of Prince Hal, and the heroic sacrifice of Hotspur at Shrewsbury are replaced with the subtle scheming of Prince John, who violates the terms of truce once the rebel army deserts its leaders. Glorious death has become ignominious capture, and daring combat, cold scheming. Prince John's claim that "God, and not we, hath safely fought today" would seem ironic were he not such a humorless young man; as it is, it seems a kind of blasphemy, if not of God, at least of Shrewsbury. Even the comic episode of the battle, Falstaff's taking Coleville of the dale as prisoner, rapidly turns grim, as Falstaff's banter with his prize is interrupted by Prince John's summary sentencing of Coleville to death. There is a sense throughout the play of history repeating itself, but more wearily and numbingly with each revolution. As the king himself acknowledges, the processes of time and event are depressingly devolutionary: "The happiest youth, viewing his progress through, / What perils past, what crosses to ensue, / Would shut the book, and sit him down and die." And as Warwick replies to him, there is nothing new under the sun: "There is a history in all men's lives, / Figuring the nature of the times deceased, / The which observed, a man may prophesy, / With a near aim, of the main chance of things / As yet not come to life." *Plus ça change* . . . Politics is no longer a matter of high ideals and high tempers, but an ignoble and repetitive motion of declining momentum.

This sense of mind-numbing devolution infects the sense of the political world at large. It is, as all acknowledge, a diseased world, from the highest echelons to the lowest. If Prince John disappoints the glorious expectations of honorable battle, Hostess Quickly, without imagination, breaks the law against meat-eating in Lent: "All victuallers do so. What's a joint of mutton or two in a whole Lent?" This lazy and sliding transgression is a far cry from the inventive double robbery at Gad's Hill, and indicates that the turgid wars of kings and noblemen have infected all of society, encouraging a kind of venal conformity to the lowest common denominator of civil behavior. (By the end of the play such petty venality has turned quite vicious indeed, when a man dies of a beating administered by Mistress Quickly, Doll Common, and Pistol.) The lower order mimics the high, and vice versa, a Bardolph in each. The tavern and the seat of country justice are uncomfortably similar sites of drunken revelry.

Accompanying this sense of pervasive civil disease is an

epidemic sense of nepotism in power relations. All members of this society trade upon their prospective connections to the powerful. As the prince scoffs, "Nay, they will be kin to us, or they will fetch it from Japeth." Falstaff claims that Poins puts it about that the prince will marry his sister; he himself is banking on his connection to the prince in order to coax a loan from Justice Shallow, and the latter alternates between boasting that he "is, sir, under the king, in some authority," dropping the name of the long-dead John of Gaunt (Hal's grandfather), and hoping that Falstaff's connection to the prince will secure his future hopes. Justice Shallow's servants, meanwhile, intercede with their master for confirmed villains (an abuse that shocks even Falstaff). This is a world that lacks and craves an impersonal, abstract law, unbendable by circumstance or acquaintance, and while all of its inhabitants recognize the corrosive and sordid effects of its absence, none seem able to institute one.

Accompanying this need for an unyielding justice is a desire for change, some way to shrug off the homogenizing cycles of corruption and corrosion that have come to dominate events like a kind of political quicksand. But such a possibility seems futile. When Hostess Quickly seeks to sue Falstaff for unpaid bills and breach of promise, we almost hope for her success, such would be the novelty of that action; when she succumbs to Falstaff's same tired promises of reparation, we wearily recognize the pattern. So too Lady Percy, Hotspur's widow, argues for some interruption of the pattern of war ("O, yet for God's sake, go not to these wars!"), but she does so by urging her father-in-law to repeat his earlier failure to second the rebel troops. Hal seizes the crown, but then must return it.

One might think that the tavern world would thrive in an atmosphere of lawlessness such as this, but it's as if it cannot carry on with the same brio once it lacks a law against which to strive. (As Prince Hal remarked in *1*

Henry IV, "If all the year were playing holidays, / To sport would be as tedious as to work.") The tavern milieu, by sheer familiarity, has lost its originality, like a too-oft-told joke; it has become both an echo of its former self and merely a rendition of other forms of social disorder, a repeat performance in every sense. This is most apparent in Falstaff himself. The vitality, energetic wordplay, and improvisational mockery of power that endeared him to us earlier have dwindled to a few stale jokes about his girth. Presumably the popularity of Falstaff in *1 Henry IV* accounts in part for Shakespeare's structuring his sequence as he does, with an entire play devoted to the continuing civil unrest after the climax of Shrewsbury, and the prolonged wait for Henry IV's death and Prince Hal's conversion and accession. But it is as if Falstaff himself is weary of the notoriety that has earned him this encore: "The brain of this foolish compounded clay-man is not able to invent anything that intends to laughter more than I invent or is invented on me." He has, as he knows, become a kind of cliché. His jokes are not as keen, nor his will to live as audacious. Instead, there is both an acknowledgment of his age ("I am old, I am old") and a querulous fear of his ultimate demise: "Peace, good Doll! Do not speak like a death's-head. Do not bid me remember mine end." The company he keeps similarly lacks animation, its members too drunk or distracted to join together in concerted fun.

Tellingly, where before, in *1 Henry IV,* we impatiently awaited Falstaff's appearance and bombast, now we anticipate Prince Hal's arrival, as if only the synergy of the two will spark the former levity. As the third drawer anticipates when the prince and Poins appear in the Eastcheap tavern, "By the mass, here will be old Utis." But as soon as Hal and Falstaff are reunited and begin, haltingly, to trade a few good jokes, the summons to war arrives, and the fun is interrupted. As Falstaff complains, "now comes in the sweetest morsel of the night, and we must hence and leave it unpicked." Our hopes of such sweetness are left at that. Throughout the play Shakespeare teases us with, and frustrates us of, the prospect of Hal and Falstaff's reunion, and this initial foreclosure foreshadows the final one.

Indeed, Falstaff seems to spend more time bantering with Prince John than he does with his "tender lambkin." Such is the index of Hal's elusiveness in the play generally. Whereas in *1 Henry IV* we see him in soliloquy, confiding to us his (rather unappealing) plan to use the tavern company as a foil for his own "reformation," here we wait largely in vain for glimpses of the profligate prince, who spends much of his time offstage. When he appears, we see a young man who seems to lack his former Machiavellian edge. His first words in the play are "Before God, I am exceeding weary." What he seems largely weary *of* is his own well-wrought myth of dissipation. He seems to doubt the success of his plan in *1 Henry IV*, to "falsify men's hopes" in "Redeeming time when men think least I will" (*1 Henry IV*, I.2.203-10). He has, it seems, played his part only too well. Despite his success at Shrewsbury, Prince Henry is unable to escape the role he has crafted for himself, and his father is as despairing of his future as ever: "The blood weeps from my heart when I do shape / In forms imaginary th' unguided days / And rotten time that you shall look upon / When I am sleeping with my ancestors." When Prince Henry repents to his father of his haste to seize the crown, he may indeed be sincere – his father is certainly persuaded – but we have seen this scene played beforetimes, and Henry IV seems as easily placated by his son as Hostess Quickly is by Falstaff.

The irony of course is that Hal may well be sincere, but it is long past the moment when he could be believed to be so. (Warwick, for one, is on to him: "The prince will in the perfectness of time / Cast off his followers.") In this world in which history seems to repeat itself ever more feebly, where hopes are false and reputations are both too fixed and yet fleeting, it hardly seems to matter. (Warwick himself may not believe his words, which are uttered to comfort the king.) The problem in this universe is that sincerity of speech or action – in the sense of originality and authenticity – is long gone, eroded by the climate of ever feebler echoes of long-lost first truths. The play opens, unusually for Shakespeare, with the chorus figure of Rumor, who describes the climate he will govern: one of "continual slanders," "False reports," "surmises, jealousies, conjectures." Expectations and hopes, disappointments and fears, prophecies and warnings abound, but not positive events, not in prospect and nearly not in retrospect. Whether it is the number of enemy forces, the record of Falstaff's deeds at Shrewsbury, or the fear of Henry V's debauchery, no single certain standard of truth applies, "consent upon a sure foundation." Rather, as Lord Bardolph warns, "we fortify in paper and in figures." We are far from the history of truth and fact, a providential record of divine meanings enacted through human lives, and plunged instead into a bewildering circuit of competing versions and visions.

Seeking to escape this circuit, and return to a sense of lineal order and priority, where myths – like that of the divine right of kings – had the power to compel belief, Henry IV tells his son that the crown "Falls upon thee in a more fairer sort" than it did to him, and "So thou the garland wear'st successively." Hal, too, in speaking to the crown, shares the fantasy that his is a more divine right than his father's had been: "Which, as immediate from thy place and blood, / Derives itself to me . . . this lineal honor." But we well know that such sacred claims have been long superseded in this universe by quite another kind of power: "now the bishop turns insurrection to religion." Tellingly, Henry IV thinks, according to a prophecy, that he is to die in Jerusalem, as indeed he is – in a room of his palace named so. It is a fulfillment that brilliantly figures the loss of the former sacred truths and their replacement by the far more mundane terms of realpolitik. "Jerusalem" has always meant the latter to Henry IV; as he has tried throughout his reign to redirect civil broils toward the Holy Land, he urges his son on his deathbed "to busy giddy minds / With foreign quarrels."

In such a universe, devoid of sacred truth, information is always misinformation. The play is filled with misprisions, and progresses from the puncturing of one false hope or fear to the construction of another, to be deflated in turn. The play opens with Northumberland's misapprehension of the result at Shrewsbury and his son's demise. Most of the other miscalculations, of course, turn on the fate of Prince Hal: such as the king's about his own son; the Lord Chief Justice's, concerning his own fate at the hands of Henry V ("which cannot look more hideously upon me / Than I have drawn it in my fantasy"); and finally, achingly, Falstaff's, about his reunion with "Harry the Fifth." The repeated correction of hopes is perhaps an apt structure for a history play, in which, of course, we always know before the characters do what their fates will be. But nowhere in Shakespeare's work is the dramatic irony as pervasive or as painful. At every turn, we are denied suspense.

Such a deliberate withholding on Shakespeare's part lends to our experience of the play's various episodes a kind of weariness, or jadedness, a kind of exhaustion with our own relentless prescience. We begin to crave some reversal of the pattern of our foreknowledge. At the same time we yearn for the final dénouement, where all the characters will finally catch up to our own knowledge of their outcomes. In the rejection of Falstaff, Shakespeare satisfies both these desires, simultaneously. But he does so in a manner that makes us regret we have ever yearned for them. Having wearied us with the sordid nature of this political world, with repetitions that never seem to advance anything but the passage of time, with cliché, with venial political and personal sins, with the abuse of justice, the abuse of reputation, with old men, with making us beg for the reformation that has so long titillated us that we have virtually lost the desire for it, for something *new,* Shakespeare makes us repent of our own impatience, with a vengeance that seems close to cruelty.

The rejection of Falstaff by Henry V may be the most painful moment in Shakespeare. "I know thee not, old man" – the line is a virtual archetype of emotional savagery. It is a pain that all our preparation, foreknowledge, and impatient anticipation only render us the more unready to suffer. Ironically, our unreadiness is partly due to the fact that this is the one piece of this history (or "necessity," as the king terms it) that we almost manage to forget we must remember. And this despite the fact that two scenes prior to the final encounter of King Henry V with his former companion, the new king has surprised another old man, the Lord Chief Justice, by reinvesting him with the very law that he had seemed to flout, "With this remembrance, that you use the same / With the like bold, just and impartial spirit / As you have done 'gainst me." We ought to know better.

Why does the reversal of Falstaff's expectations come, then, if not as a surprise, then as such a painful recognition? The answer must lie partly in Gloucestershire, that land of wine and roses (or sack and pippins). Gloucestershire *is* something new in this Henriad world: the two scenes set there are the only portions of this play not indebted to Shakespeare's chronicle record or crucial to the advancement of the plot. Gloucestershire is, as King Lear sardonically remarks of old age, "unnecessary"; and it also serves as the one place where we can experience old age, nostalgia, and the past with something other than the impatience with which we greet them everywhere else in this play. It is a site akin to the tavern, insofar as drinking and storytelling take place there, but it is as if the sins of Eastcheap become innocent in the good country air. Even the pecunious impressment of the comically reluctant soldiers Mouldy, Wart, Feeble, Shadow, and Bullcalf seems gently scurrilous here rather than cynically rapacious.

Interestingly, Falstaff at first seems impatient himself with the elderliness of its denizens, and indignant with their comparative prosperity. Shallow and Silence are forgetful, nostalgic, morbid, given to interminable reminiscences about long dead people we've never met and odd questions about the price of ewes. They are like elderly relatives whom we must, out of duty, humor, but who we really don't believe were ever young (Falstaff, a boy?!), and we wish they would come to what we think is the point and let us go about our business. Falstaff's first reaction to Shallow is one of disbelief and jealousy, that such a poor excuse for a youthful gallant could have garnered "lands and beefs." When he returns, however, in Act V, scene 3, in order to fleece Shallow, he gradually joins with Shallow and Silence in drink and song, amazed, as we are, at their capacity for merriness as well as morbidity ("I did not think Master Silence had been a man of this mettle"). He seems almost to forget his own weariness, and greets the news of Hal's accession with the energy of the old Falstaff (as opposed to the aged Falstaff).

These brief moments of drunken revelry move us from laughing at, to laughing with, old men, as they sing the songs of their youth, and hear the chimes at midnight once again. Or almost so; it is, at least, as close as we get in this play to forgetting our impatience for the future – to forgetting, with these old men, even if in drink, death. For a brief moment we see old age as less indecorous than the scorn for it. Earlier comments such as Poins's on Falstaff's aged lechery – "Is it not strange that desire should so many years outlive performance?" – appear in this midnight light callous rather than witty. For a moment, we view these "withered elders" with something other than pity or irritation or disgust, and their critics seem nothing so much as rude puppies. In Falstaff's earlier estimate of Poins – that the prince loves him "because their legs are both of a bigness, and a plays at quoits well, . . . and jumps upon joint stools, and swears with good grace, and wears his boots very smooth, . . . and such other gambol faculties a has that show a weak mind and an able body" – we hear not jealousy but the pain of a friend forsaken for the simple reason that he is out of fashion. The singing of these old men suggests that, tragically, desire only increases as performance declines, and perhaps for a moment we view that fact not with contempt or loathing but with a kind of shared sentimentality for the end to which we must all come, for we all, "bona robas," or no, "cannot choose but be old." In Act V, scene 3, we suspend, however briefly, belief, and forget fact.

Thus it is that, having been lost in rural revelry, when we come to Falstaff's reunion with his king we are all the more unprepared for it. For while it may be true that Falstaff is old, fat, scurrilous, disreputable, shabbily dressed, and looking forward to capitalizing on his friendship with "Harry the Fifth," it is also equally true that he loves the new king. He loves to talk of him, and with him; he spends time thinking of ways to amuse him ("I will devise matter enough out of this Shallow to keep Prince Harry in continual laughter the wearing out of six fashions"); he measures Hal's feelings for him by his own for the prince: "I know the young king is sick for me." To the prince, meanwhile, Falstaff is the "fat villain," "the martlemas," "this wen," and most cruelly, "old man." Falstaff spends the play waiting for his time with the prince, but the distance kept between them throughout does nothing to mitigate the final blow, and only increases his anticipation in their reunion: "God save thee, my sweet boy!" "God save thy grace, King Hal, my royal Hal! My king!" "My Jove! I speak to thee, my heart!" We feel his rejection all the more strongly both because we have ourselves wished it at times, but also because we too would cherish the fantasy that Jack will have Hal again, and all will be well. The public nature of the king's denial adds to Falstaff's humiliation, and the emphasis on the prospect of the gaping grave, "For thee thrice wider than for other men," – that which Falstaff at his best helps us all forget – seems gratuitously cruel. This event is a necessity, yes, and a foregone conclusion; but much like death we would prefer to forget it, and we joy in those who allow us to do so. Marx wrote that history repeats itself, the first time as tragedy, the second time, farce. For all its repetitions, *2 Henry IV* ultimately reverses the maxim.

CLAIRE MCEACHERN
University of California at Los Angeles

Note on the Text

THE PRESENT EDITION is based on the quarto of 1600, which is believed to have been printed from Shakespeare's own manuscript and to supply a better text than the folio, although that of the latter is fuller. The list of characters has been added from the folio text, as well as certain passages evidently omitted from the quarto because they dwell at length upon the censorable subject of civil rebellion. (These are the bracketed lines I.1, 167-80, 190-210; I.3, 21-24, 36-55, 85-108; II.3, 23-45; IV.1, 55-79, 103-39.) The quarto is not divided into acts and scenes, and the division here indicated is that of the folio text, except that in the latter the first act contains five scenes owing to the Induction's being counted as a separate scene, and the fourth act contains only two scenes. The wording of the stage directions of the quarto has been retained, but the names of four characters who neither speak nor are referred to in the dialogue have been eliminated: "Fauconbridge" in the opening stage direction at I.3; "Sir John Russell" in that at II.2; "Bardolph" in that at IV.1; and "Kent" in that at IV.4. In V.4, "Sincklo" (presumably the actor taking the part) has been emended to "Beadle." Listed below are substantive departures from the quarto text, including additions from the folio other than those mentioned above. The adopted reading is given in italics followed by the quarto reading in roman.

The Actors' Names (printed at the end of the play in F)
Ind. *Induction* (i.e., the heading, F; omitted in Q)   **35** *hold* (Theobald) hole (F; passage not in Q)
I.1   127 *Too* (F) so   **162** TRAVERS (Capell) Umfr.   **165** *Lean on your* (F)

leaue on you   179 *brought* (F2) bring (F; passage not in Q)   184 *ventured, . . . proposed* (Capell) ventured . . . proposde,

I.2   20 *fledged* (F) fledge   35 *rascally* (F) rascal!   47 *Where's Bardolph?* (F; follows "through it" in line above in Q)   48 *into* (F) in   94 *age* (F) an ague   117 *Falstaff* (F) Old.   166 *bearherd* (F) Berod   169 *them, are* (F) the one   169 *and Prince Harry* (F; omitted in Q)

I.3   28 *on* (F) and   66 *a* (F) so,   79 *He . . . Welsh* (F) French and Welch he leaues his back vnarmde, they   109 *Mowbray* (F) Bish.

II.1   14 *and that* (F; omitted in Q)   21 *vice* (F) view   25 *continuantly* (F) continually   78 *Fie!* (F; omitted in Q)   161 **s.d.** (follows l. 158 in Q)   165 *Basingstoke* (F) Billingsgate

II.2   15 *viz.* (F) with   21 *thy* (F) the; *made a shift to* (F; omitted in Q)   78 *new* (F; omitted in Q)   81 *rabbit* (F) rabble   109 *borrower's* (Warburton) borrowed   124 *familiars* (F) family

II.3   11 *endeared* (F) endeere

II.4   12–13 *Dispatch . . . straight* (F; assigned to "Dra." in Q)   13 **s.d.** (follows line 17 in Q)   14 THIRD DRAWER (Alexander) 2 Drawer (F) Francis (Q)   20 SECOND DRAWER (F) Francis   110 *shall* (F) shall not   167 *Die* (F; omitted in Q)   211 *Ah* (F) a   214 *Ah,* (F) a   313 *him* (F) thee

III.2   27 *This . . . cousin* (F) Coosin, this sir Iohn   55 [SHALLOW] . . . *gentlemen* (F; assigned to "Silence" in Q)   110 FALSTAFF *Prick him* (F; printed as s.d. "Iohn prickes him" after line 109 in Q)   134 *to* (F; omitted in Q)   194–95 *no more of that* (F; omitted in Q)   207 *Clement's Inn* (F) Clemham   226 *old* (F; omitted in Q)   282 *Master Shallow* (F; omitted in Q)

IV.1   30 *Then, my lord* (F; omitted in Q)   34 *rags* (F) rage   139 *indeed* (Theobald) and did (F; passage not in Q)

IV.2   **s.d.** (follows IV.1.226 in Q)   8 *man* (F) man talking   24 *Employ* (F) Imply   97 **s.d.** (follows line 96 in Q)   117 *and . . . yours* (F; omitted in Q)   122 *these traitors* (F) this traitour

IV.3   2 *I pray* (F; omitted in Q)   40 *their* (Q catchword) there   41 *Caesar* (Theobald) cosin   80–84 (printed as prose in Q)   82 *pray,* (F; omitted in Q)

IV.4   32 *meting* (F) meeting   52 *Canst . . . that?* (F; omitted in Q)   94 *heaven* (F) heavens   104 *write* (F) wet; *letters* (F) termes   132 *Softly, pray* (F; omitted in Q)

IV.5   13 *altered* (F) uttred   49 *How . . . grace?* (F; omitted in Q)   75 *The virtuous sweets* (F; omitted in Q)   81 *hath* (F) hands   107 *Which* (F) Whom   160 *worst of* (F) worse then   177 *O my son,* (F; omitted in Q)

V.1   22 *the other day* (F; omitted in Q)   *Hinckley* (F) Hunkley   45 *but a very* (F; omitted in Q)

V.2   **s.d.** ("duke Humphrey, Thomas Clarence, Prince John, Westmerland" also listed in Q)

V.3   17–22, 32–36, 46–48, 53–54, 73–75, 92–96, 99–106, 115–19, 126–27, 139–41 (printed as prose in Q)

V.4   5 *enough* (F; omitted in Q)   6 *lately* (F; omitted in Q)   12 *He* (F) I

V.5   5 *Robert* (F; omitted in Q)   15 SHALLOW (F) Pist.   17, 19 SHALLOW (Hanmer) Pist.   29 *all* (F; omitted in Q)   31–38 (printed as prose in Q)

Epi.   30–31 *and . . . queen* (F; follows line 14 in Q)

The Second Part of King Henry the Fourth

THE ACTORS' NAMES

RUMOR, *the Presenter*

KING HENRY THE FOURTH

PRINCE HENRY, *afterwards crowned King Henry the Fifth*

PRINCE JOHN OF LANCASTER ⎫
HUMPHREY OF GLOUCESTER ⎬ *sons to Henry IV and*
THOMAS OF CLARENCE   ⎭ *brethren to Henry V*

[EARL OF] NORTHUMBERLAND

[RICHARD SCROOP,] THE ARCHBISHOP OF YORK ⎫
[LORD] MOWBRAY   ⎪
[LORD] HASTINGS ⎪ *against*
LORD BARDOLPH   ⎬ *King*
TRAVERS   ⎪ *Henry*
MORTON   ⎪ *IV*
[SIR JOHN] COLEVILLE ⎭

[EARL OF] WARWICK   ⎫
[EARL OF] WESTMORELAND ⎪
[EARL OF] SURREY   ⎪
[SIR JOHN BLUNT]   ⎪
GOWER   ⎬ *of the king's party*
HARCOURT   ⎪
LORD CHIEF JUSTICE   ⎪
[HIS SERVANT]   ⎭

[ROBERT] SHALLOW ⎫ *both country justices*
SILENCE   ⎭

DAVY, *servant to Shallow*

FANG AND SNARE, *two sergeants*

[RALPH] MOULDY   ⎫
[SIMON] SHADOW   ⎪
[THOMAS] WART   ⎬ *country soldiers*
[FRANCIS] FEEBLE ⎪
[PETER] BULLCALF ⎭

POINS
[SIR JOHN] FALSTAFF
BARDOLPH
PISTOL
PETO } *tavern denizens*
[FALSTAFF'S] PAGE
HOSTESS QUICKLY
DOLL TEARSHEET
NORTHUMBERLAND'S WIFE
PERCY'S WIDOW [LADY PERCY]
[A DANCER AS] EPILOGUE
[FRANCIS AND OTHER] DRAWERS, BEADLE [AND OTHER
    OFFICERS], GROOMS [, PORTER, MESSENGER,
    SOLDIERS, LORDS, ATTENDANTS]

[SCENE: *England*]
*

The Second Part of King
Henry the Fourth

ॐ Induction

Enter Rumor, painted full of tongues.

RUMOR
Open your ears, for which of you will stop   1
The vent of hearing when loud Rumor speaks?
I, from the orient to the drooping west,
Making the wind my post horse, still unfold   4
The acts commencèd on this ball of earth.
Upon my tongues continual slanders ride,
The which in every language I pronounce,
Stuffing the ears of men with false reports.
I speak of peace while covert enmity
Under the smile of safety wounds the world.   10
And who but Rumor, who but only I,
Make fearful musters and prepared defense   12
Whiles the big year, swol'n with some other grief,   13
Is thought with child by the stern tyrant war,   14
And no such matter? Rumor is a pipe   15
Blown by surmises, jealousies, conjectures,
And of so easy and so plain a stop   17

Ind. 1 *stop* block   **4** *post horse* horse ridden between inns, or post houses, by travelers; *still* ever   **12** *musters* gatherings of soldiers   **13** *big* swollen   **14** *with child* pregnant   **15** *no such matter* not the case; *pipe* wind instrument   **17** *of . . . stop* whose stops, or note holes, are so easily played upon

18   That the blunt monster with uncounted heads,
       The still-discordant wavering multitude,
20   Can play upon it. But what need I thus
21   My well-known body to anatomize
22   Among my household? Why is Rumor here?
       I run before King Harry's victory,
       Who in a bloody field by Shrewsbury
25   Hath beaten down young Hotspur and his troops,
       Quenching the flame of bold rebellion
       Even with the rebels' blood. But what mean I
28   To speak so true at first? My office is
29   To noise about that Harry Monmouth fell
30   Under the wrath of noble Hotspur's sword,
       And that the king before the Douglas' rage
       Stooped his anointed head as low as death.
33   This have I rumored through the peasant towns
       Between that royal field of Shrewsbury
35   And this worm-eaten hold of ragged stone,
       Where Hotspur's father, old Northumberland,
37   Lies crafty-sick. The posts come tiring on,
       And not a man of them brings other news
       Than they have learned of me. From Rumor's tongues
40   They bring smooth comforts false, worse than true
       wrongs.   *Exit Rumor.*

*

---

18 *blunt . . . heads* the Hydra, or many-headed monster (a term used to describe the populace)   **21** *anatomize* display, enumerate   **22** *household* i.e., the audience   **25** *Hotspur* Harry Percy, killed in the recent battle at Shrewsbury by Prince Henry   **28** *office* job, role   **29** *noise about* spread word; *Harry Monmouth* Prince Henry (born at Monmouth, in Wales)   **33** *peasant towns* villages   **35** *hold* castle, stronghold (Warkworth Castle, seat of the Earl of Northumberland, Hotspur's father)   **37** *crafty-sick* pretending illness; *posts* messengers; *tiring on* riding to exhaustion

∾ **I.1** *Enter the Lord Bardolph at one door.*

LORD BARDOLPH
  Who keeps the gate here, ho?   1
    [Enter the Porter.]   Where is the earl?
PORTER
  What shall I say you are?   2
LORD BARDOLPH   Tell thou the earl
  That the Lord Bardolph doth attend him here.   3
PORTER
  His lordship is walked forth into the orchard.
  Please it your honor, knock but at the gate,
  And he himself will answer.
    Enter the Earl of Northumberland.
LORD BARDOLPH   Here comes the earl.
                                      [Exit Porter.]

NORTHUMBERLAND
  What news, Lord Bardolph? Every minute now
  Should be the father of some stratagem.   8
  The times are wild. Contention, like a horse
  Full of high feeding, madly hath broke loose   10
  And bears down all before him.
LORD BARDOLPH   Noble earl,
  I bring you certain news from Shrewsbury.
NORTHUMBERLAND
  Good, an God will!   13
LORD BARDOLPH   As good as heart can wish.
  The king is almost wounded to the death;
  And, in the fortune of my lord your son,   15
  Prince Harry slain outright; and both the Blunts
  Killed by the hand of Douglas. Young Prince John

I.1 At the gate of Northumberland's castle at Warkworth 1 *keeps* guards
2 *What* who 3 *attend him* await him 8 *stratagem* violent deed 10 *high
feeding* over-rich feed 13 *an God will* God willing 15 *in the fortune of*
as for the fate of, or due to the luck of

And Westmoreland and Stafford fled the field;
19 And Harry Monmouth's brawn, the hulk Sir John,
20 Is prisoner to your son. O, such a day,
So fought, so followed, and so fairly won,
Came not till now to dignify the times
23 Since Caesar's fortunes!
NORTHUMBERLAND   How is this derived?
Saw you the field? Came you from Shrewsbury?
LORD BARDOLPH
I spake with one, my lord, that came from thence,
A gentleman well bred and of good name,
27 That freely rendered me these news for true.
NORTHUMBERLAND
Here comes my servant Travers, whom I sent
On Tuesday last to listen after news.
Enter Travers.
LORD BARDOLPH
30 My lord, I overrode him on the way,
31 And he is furnished with no certainties
32 More than he haply may retail from me.
NORTHUMBERLAND
Now, Travers, what good tidings comes with you?
TRAVERS
34 My lord, Sir John Umfrevile turned me back
With joyful tidings, and, being better horsed,
Outrode me. After him came spurring hard
37 A gentleman, almost forspent with speed,
38 That stopped by me to breathe his bloodied horse.
He asked the way to Chester, and of him
40 I did demand what news from Shrewsbury.
He told me that rebellion had bad luck
And that young Harry Percy's spur was cold.

---

19 *brawn* boar   **23** *fortunes* victories; *derived* come by   **27** *rendered* delivered to   **31** *furnished* provided   **32** *haply* perhaps; *retail* relate   **34** *Sir John Umfrevile* originally Lord Bardolph in an earlier version of this scene?   **37** *forspent* exhausted   **38** *breathe* let catch breath

With that, he gave his able horse the head,
And bending forward struck his armèd heels   44
Against the panting sides of his poor jade   45
Up to the rowel head, and starting so   46
He seemed in running to devour the way,
Staying no longer question.   48

NORTHUMBERLAND   Ha! Again.
Said he young Harry Percy's spur was cold?
Of Hotspur Coldspur? That rebellion   50
Had met ill luck?

LORD BARDOLPH   My lord, I'll tell you what.
If my young lord your son have not the day,   52
Upon mine honor, for a silken point   53
I'll give my barony. Never talk of it.

NORTHUMBERLAND
Why should that gentleman that rode by Travers
Give then such instances of loss?

LORD BARDOLPH   Who, he?
He was some hilding fellow that had stolen   57
The horse he rode on, and, upon my life,
Spoke at a venture. Look, here comes more news.   59

    Enter Morton.

NORTHUMBERLAND
Yea, this man's brow, like to a title leaf,   60
Foretells the nature of a tragic volume.
So looks the strand whereon the imperious flood   62
Hath left a witnessed usurpation.   63
Say, Morton, didst thou come from Shrewsbury?

MORTON
I ran from Shrewsbury, my noble lord,
Where hateful death put on his ugliest mask
To fright our party.

----

44 *armed* i.e., spurred   45 *jade* nag   46 *rowel head* the spiked wheel of a
spur   48 *staying no* not waiting for   52 *have not the day* has not carried the
day, won the battle   53 *point* fastening lace   57 *hilding* worthless, low-rate
59 *at a venture* carelessly, without foundation   60 *title leaf* i.e., of a book
62 *strand* riverbank   63 *witnessed usurpation* sign of flooding

NORTHUMBERLAND   How doth my son and brother?
    Thou tremblest, and the whiteness in thy cheek
70 Is apter than thy tongue to tell thy errand.
    Even such a man, so faint, so spiritless,
    So dull, so dead in look, so woebegone,
73 Drew Priam's curtain in the dead of night,
    And would have told him half his Troy was burnt.
    But Priam found the fire ere he his tongue,
    And I my Percy's death ere thou report'st it.
    This thou wouldst say, "Your son did thus and thus;
    Your brother thus. So fought the noble Douglas" –
79 Stopping my greedy ear with their bold deeds.
80 But in the end, to stop my ear indeed,
    Thou hast a sigh to blow away this praise,
    Ending with "Brother, son, and all are dead."
MORTON
    Douglas is living, and your brother, yet;
    But, for my lord your son –
NORTHUMBERLAND   Why, he is dead.
    See what a ready tongue suspicion hath!
    He that but fears the thing he would not know
    Hath by instinct knowledge from others' eyes
88 That what he feared is chancèd. Yet speak, Morton.
89 Tell thou an earl his divination lies,
90 And I will take it as a sweet disgrace
    And make thee rich for doing me such wrong.
MORTON
92 You are too great to be by me gainsaid.
93 Your spirit is too true, your fears too certain.
NORTHUMBERLAND
    Yet, for all this, say not that Percy's dead.
    I see a strange confession in thine eye.
    Thou shakest thy head and hold'st it fear or sin

---

70 *apter* more able   73 *Priam* King of Troy   79 *Stopping* filling up   88
chancèd occurred   89 *divination* prophecy   92 *gainsaid* contradicted   93
spirit hunch, intuition

To speak a truth. If he be slain, say so.
The tongue offends not that reports his death;
And he doth sin that doth belie the dead,   99
Not he which says the dead is not alive.   100
Yet the first bringer of unwelcome news
Hath but a losing office, and his tongue   102
Sounds ever after as a sullen bell,
Remembered tolling a departing friend.   104

LORD BARDOLPH
I cannot think, my lord, your son is dead.

MORTON
I am sorry I should force you to believe
That which I would to God I had not seen.
But these mine eyes saw him in bloody state,
Rendering faint quittance, wearied and outbreathed,   109
To Harry Monmouth, whose swift wrath beat down   110
The never-daunted Percy to the earth,
From whence with life he never more sprung up.
In few, his death, whose spirit lent a fire   113
Even to the dullest peasant in his camp,
Being bruited once, took fire and heat away   115
From the best-tempered courage in his troops.   116
For from his metal was his party steeled,   117
Which once in him abated, all the rest
Turned on themselves, like dull and heavy lead.
And as the thing that's heavy in itself,   120
Upon enforcement flies with greatest speed,   121
So did our men, heavy in Hotspur's loss,
Lend to this weight such lightness with their fear
That arrows fled not swifter toward their aim
Than did our soldiers, aiming at their safety,
Fly from the field. Then was that noble Worcester

---

99 *belie* lie about, slander   102 *losing office* thankless task   104 *tolling* i.e.,
like a funeral bell   109 *faint quittance* feeble parrying of blows   113 *In few*
briefly   115 *bruited* reported   116 *best-tempered* hardest-forged (like steel)
117 *metal* (with a pun on "mettle")   121 *Upon enforcement* when pushed or
thrown

Too soon ta'en prisoner; and that furious Scot,
The bloody Douglas, whose well-laboring sword
129   Had three times slain the appearance of the king,
130   'Gan vail his stomach and did grace the shame
Of those that turned their backs, and in his flight,
Stumbling in fear, was took. The sum of all
Is that the king hath won, and hath sent out
A speedy power to encounter you, my lord,
135   Under the conduct of young Lancaster
And Westmoreland. This is the news at full.

NORTHUMBERLAND
For this I shall have time enough to mourn.
138   In poison there is physic; and these news,
139   Having been well, that would have made me sick,
140   Being sick, have in some measure made me well.
And as the wretch whose fever-weakened joints,
Like strengthless hinges, buckle under life,
143   Impatient of his fit, breaks like a fire
144   Out of his keeper's arms, even so my limbs,
Weakened with grief, being now enraged with grief,
146   Are thrice themselves. Hence, therefore, thou nice
        crutch!
147   A scaly gauntlet now with joints of steel
148   Must glove this hand. And hence, thou sickly quoif!
149   Thou art a guard too wanton for the head
150   Which princes, fleshed with conquest, aim to hit.
151   Now bind my brows with iron, and approach
152   The ragged'st hour that time and spite dare bring
To frown upon the enraged Northumberland!
Let heaven kiss earth! Now let not Nature's hand

---

129 *the appearance* (soldiers disguised as the king for decoy purposes)   130
'*Gan . . . stomach* began to lose courage; *grace* excuse, pardon   135 *conduct*
command   138 *physic* medicine   139 *Having been* Had I been   143 *Impatient of his fit* restless of his illness   144 *keeper's* i.e., nurse's   146 *nice* effeminate   147 *gauntlet* chain-mail glove   148 *quoif* nightcap   149 *wanton*
slight or luxurious   150 *fleshed* inflamed (from the taste of blood)   151 *approach* let approach   152 *ragged'st* harshest, roughest

Keep the wild flood confined! Let order die!
And let this world no longer be a stage
To feed contention in a lingering act.   157
But let one spirit of the first-born Cain   158
Reign in all bosoms, that, each heart being set
On bloody courses, the rude scene may end,   *160*
And darkness be the burier of the dead!
[TRAVERS]
This strainèd passion doth you wrong, my lord.   162
LORD BARDOLPH
Sweet earl, divorce not wisdom from your honor.
MORTON
The lives of all your loving complices   164
Lean on your health, the which, if you give o'er
To stormy passion, must perforce decay.
[You cast the event of war, my noble lord,
And summed the account of chance, before you said,
"Let us make head." It was your presurmise   169
That, in the dole of blows, your son might drop.   170
You knew he walked o'er perils, on an edge,
More likely to fall in than to get o'er.
You were advised his flesh was capable   173
Of wounds and scars and that his forward spirit   174
Would lift him where most trade of danger ranged.
Yet did you say, "Go forth." And none of this,
Though strongly apprehended, could restrain
The stiff-borne action. What hath then befallen,   178
Or what hath this bold enterprise brought forth,
More than that being which was like to be?]   180
LORD BARDOLPH
We all that are engagèd to this loss   181
Knew that we ventured on such dangerous seas

---

157 *lingering* drawn out, fitful 158 *spirit . . . Cain* i.e., of fratricidal murder 162 *strainèd* stressful 164 *complices* allies, partners 169 *presurmise* projection 170 *dole* chance distribution 173 *capable* possibly subject to 174 *forward* impetuous 178 *stiff-borne* doggedly pursued 180 *more . . . be* more than what you knew were possibilities 181 *engagèd to* involved in

183   That if we wrought out life 'twas ten to one.
    And yet we ventured, for the gain proposed
185   Choked the respect of likely peril feared.
    And since we are o'erset, venture again.
    Come, we will all put forth, body and goods.
MORTON
    'Tis more than time. And, my most noble lord,
    I hear for certain, and dare speak the truth,
190   [The gentle Archbishop of York is up
    With well-appointed powers. He is a man
192   Who with a double surety binds his followers.
193   My lord your son had only but the corpse,
    But shadows and the shows of men, to fight.
    For that same word "rebellion" did divide
    The action of their bodies from their souls,
    And they did fight with queasiness, constrained,
    As men drink potions, that their weapons only
199   Seemed on our side. But for their spirits and souls,
200   This word "rebellion," it had froze them up,
    As fish are in a pond. But now the bishop
202   Turns insurrection to religion.
    Supposed sincere and holy in his thoughts,
    He's followed both with body and with mind,
205   And doth enlarge his rising with the blood
206   Of fair King Richard, scraped from Pomfret stones;
    Derives from heaven his quarrel and his cause;
    Tells them he doth bestride a bleeding land,
    Gasping for life under great Bolingbroke;
210   And more and less do flock to follow him.]

---

183 *wrought out life* survived, escaped with our lives   **185** *Choked the respect* outweighed the prospect   **190** *up* up in arms   **192** *double surety* bond, guarantee, certainty   **193** *corpse* material bodies   **199** *But for* but as for   **202** *Turns . . . religion* makes rebellion a spiritual cause   **205** *enlarge his rising* enhance the cause of his uprising   **206** *Pomfret* (the castle where Richard II was murdered by order of Henry Bolingbroke, King Henry IV)   **210** *more and less* persons of great and low birth

NORTHUMBERLAND
  I knew of this before; but, to speak truth,
  This present grief had wiped it from my mind.
  Go in with me, and counsel every man
  The aptest way for safety and revenge.
  Get posts and letters, and make friends with speed.   215
  Never so few, and never yet more need.   *Exeunt.*

∗

∿ **I.2** *Enter Sir John [Falstaff] alone, with his Page*
  bearing his sword and buckler.

FALSTAFF   Sirrah, you giant, what says the doctor to my   1
  water?   2
PAGE   He said, sir, the water itself was a good healthy
  water; but, for the party that owed it, he might have   4
  moe diseases than he knew for.   5
FALSTAFF   Men of all sorts take a pride to gird at me. The   6
  brain of this foolish compounded clay-man is not able
  to invent anything that intends to laughter more than I   8
  invent or is invented on me. I am not only witty in myself, but the cause that wit is in other men. I do here   10
  walk before thee like a sow that hath overwhelmed all   11
  her litter but one. If the prince put thee into my service
  for any other reason than to set me off, why then I have   13
  no judgment. Thou whoreson mandrake, thou art fit-   14
  ter to be worn in my cap than to wait at my heels. I was
  never manned with an agate till now. But I will inset   16
  you neither in gold nor silver, but in vile apparel, and   17
  send you back again to your master, for a jewel – the   18

---

215 *posts* messengers; *make* summon, collect
  I.2 A London street 1 *giant* (ironically, as the page is small) 2 *water*
  urine, examined to determine the health of its owner 4 *owed* owned 5
  moe more 6 *gird at* taunt 8 *intends to* solicits 11 *overwhelmed* crushed
  13 *set me off* annoy me 14 *whoreson* son of a whore; *mandrake* a forked root
  supposed to resemble a man 16 *agate* a stone carved with small figures 17
  vile low-born 18 *for a jewel* as if you were a jewel

19   juvenal, the prince your master, whose chin is not yet
20   fledged. I will sooner have a beard grow in the palm of
       my hand than he shall get one off his cheek, and yet he
22   will not stick to say his face is a face-royal. God may
       finish it when he will, 'tis not a hair amiss yet. He may
       keep it still at a face-royal, for a barber shall never earn
       sixpence out of it; and yet he'll be crowing as if he had
26   writ man ever since his father was a bachelor. He may
27   keep his own grace, but he's almost out of mine, I can
       assure him. What said Master Dombledon about the
29   satin for my short cloak and my slops?

30   PAGE   He said, sir, you should procure him better assur-
31   ance than Bardolph. He would not take his band and
       yours; he liked not the security.

33   FALSTAFF   Let him be damned, like the glutton! Pray
34   God his tongue be hotter! A whoreson Achitophel! A
35   rascally yea-forsooth knave! To bear a gentleman in
       hand, and then stand upon security! The whoreson
37   smooth-pates do now wear nothing but high shoes, and
38   bunches of keys at their girdles; and if a man is through
       with them in honest taking up, then they must stand
40   upon security. I had as lief they would put ratsbane in
41   my mouth as offer to stop it with security. I looked a
       should have sent me two-and-twenty yards of satin, as I
       am a true knight, and he sends me security. Well, he

---

19 *juvenal* young man   20 *fledged* feathered with a downy beard   22 *stick to* stop from claiming; *face-royal* (a pun derived from the royal, a coin worth ten shillings with the king's face stamped on it)   26 *writ man* signed himself as a man   27 *grace* (1) title (as in "your grace"), (2) favor   29 *slops* wide breeches   31 *Bardolph* a crony of Falstaff's, who shares only his name with Lord Bardolph, of the previous scene; *band* bond   33 *the glutton* (see Luke 16:24, from the parable of the rich man Dives, who in hell wished for a drop of water on his tongue from the poor man Lazarus, whom he had failed to relieve in life)   34 *Achitophel* (the treacherous advisor of Absalom, 2 Samuel 16:21)   35 *yea-forsooth knave* yes-man   35–36 *bear . . . security* encourage, and then make an issue over credit   37 *smooth-pates* city tradesmen; *high shoes* token of prosperity   38–40 *if . . . security* has agreed with them in an honest bargain, then they stipulate credit   40 *lief* rather; *ratsbane* poison   41 *a* he

may sleep in security, for he hath the horn of abun- 44
dance, and the lightness of his wife shines through it. 45
And yet cannot he see, though he have his own lan-
thorn to light him. Where's Bardolph?

PAGE   He's gone into Smithfield to buy your worship a 48
horse.

FALSTAFF   I bought him in Paul's, and he'll buy me a 50
horse in Smithfield. An I could get me but a wife in the
stews, I were manned, horsed, and wived. 52

  Enter Lord Chief Justice [and Servant].

PAGE   Sir, here comes the nobleman that committed the 53
prince for striking him about Bardolph.

FALSTAFF   Wait close; I will not see him. 55

CHIEF JUSTICE   What's he that goes there?

SERVANT   Falstaff, an't please your lordship.

CHIEF JUSTICE   He that was in question for the robbery? 58

SERVANT   He, my lord. But he hath since done good service at Shrewsbury, and, as I hear, is now going with 60
some charge to the Lord John of Lancaster. 61

CHIEF JUSTICE   What, to York? Call him back again.

SERVANT   Sir John Falstaff!

FALSTAFF   Boy, tell him I am deaf.

PAGE   You must speak louder; my master is deaf.

CHIEF JUSTICE   I am sure he is, to the hearing of anything good. Go, pluck him by the elbow; I must speak
with him.

SERVANT   Sir John!

FALSTAFF   What! A young knave, and begging! Is there 70
not wars? Is there not employment? Doth not the king
lack subjects? Do not the rebels need soldiers? Though

44–45 *horn of abundance* i.e., of a cuckold, a man whose wife is unfaithful
(cuckolds were depicted as having horns)   45 *lightness* i.e., easiness   48
Smithfield a famous livestock market   50 *Paul's* Saint Paul's Cathedral (the
nave of which served as a labor exchange)   52 *stews* houses of prostitution
53 *committed* i.e., to prison   55 *close* nearby   58 *in question* under judicial
examination; *the robbery* i.e., at Gad's Hill (see *1 Henry IV,* II.4)   61 *charge*
command of soldiers

it be a shame to be on any side but one, it is worse
shame to beg than to be on the worst side, were it worse
75 than the name of rebellion can tell how to make it.
76 SERVANT You mistake me, sir.
    FALSTAFF Why, sir, did I say you were an honest man?
78 Setting my knighthood and my soldiership aside, I had
    lied in my throat if I had said so.
80 SERVANT I pray you, sir, then set your knighthood and
81 your soldiership aside and give me leave to tell you you
    lie in your throat if you say I am any other than an hon-
    est man.
84 FALSTAFF I give thee leave to tell me so! I lay aside that
    which grows to me! If thou get'st any leave of me, hang
    me; if thou tak'st leave, thou wert better be hanged. You
87 hunt counter. Hence! Avaunt!
    SERVANT Sir, my lord would speak with you.
    CHIEF JUSTICE Sir John Falstaff, a word with you.
90 FALSTAFF My good lord! God give your lordship good
    time of day. I am glad to see your lordship abroad. I
    heard say your lordship was sick. I hope your lordship
93 goes abroad by advice. Your lordship, though not clean
    past your youth, have yet some smack of age in you,
    some relish of the saltness of time in you; and I most
    humbly beseech your lordship to have a reverent care of
    your health.
    CHIEF JUSTICE Sir John, I sent for you before your expe-
    dition to Shrewsbury.
100 FALSTAFF An't please your lordship, I hear his majesty is
    returned with some discomfort from Wales.
    CHIEF JUSTICE I talk not of his majesty. You would not
    come when I sent for you.

---

75 *make* consider 76 *mistake* misunderstand 78 *Setting . . . aside* even if I
weren't a knight and a soldier (thought to be honorable) 81 *leave* permis-
sion 84–85 *that . . . me* i.e., my knighthood, part of my nature 87
counter in the reverse of the trail; *Avaunt* go away 93 *by advice* i.e., of a doctor 93–94 *clean past* hardly 100 *An't* if it

FALSTAFF And I hear, moreover, his highness is fallen into this same whoreson apoplexy.

CHIEF JUSTICE Well, God mend him! I pray you, let me speak with you.

FALSTAFF This apoplexy, as I take it, is a kind of lethargy, an't please your lordship, a kind of sleeping in the blood, a whoreson tingling.   *110*

CHIEF JUSTICE What tell you me of it? Be it as it is.

FALSTAFF It hath it original from much grief, from study *112* and perturbation of the brain. I have read the cause of his effects in Galen. It is a kind of deafness.   *114*

CHIEF JUSTICE I think you are fallen into the disease, for you hear not what I say to you.

FALSTAFF Very well, my lord, very well. Rather, an't please you, it is the disease of not listening, the malady of not marking, that I am troubled withal.

CHIEF JUSTICE To punish you by the heels would amend *120* the attention of your ears, and I care not if I do become your physician.

FALSTAFF I am as poor as Job, my lord, but not so pa- *123* tient. Your lordship may minister the potion of impris- *124* onment to me in respect of poverty; but how I should *125* be your patient to follow your prescriptions, the wise may make some dram of a scruple, or indeed a scruple *127* itself.

CHIEF JUSTICE I sent for you, when there were matters *129* against you for your life, to come speak with me.   *130*

FALSTAFF As I was then advised by my learned counsel in the laws of this land-service, I did not come.   *132*

---

112 *it original* its cause   114 *Galen* (Greek medical authority)   120 *by the heels* in the stocks   123 *Job* (biblical figure of great suffering and patience) 124 *minister* administer   125 *in respect* on account of (he claims he is too poor to pay any fine)   127 *some . . . scruple* hesitate to admit (dram and scruple are small apothecary – pharmacist – weights)   129–30 *matters against you* charges that carried a death penalty   132 *land-service* military service

CHIEF JUSTICE Well, the truth is, Sir John, you live in great infamy.

FALSTAFF He that buckles himself in my belt cannot live in less.

137 CHIEF JUSTICE Your means are very slender and your waste is great.

FALSTAFF I would it were otherwise. I would my means
140 were greater and my waist slenderer.

CHIEF JUSTICE You have misled the youthful prince.

FALSTAFF The young prince hath misled me. I am the fellow with the great belly, and he my dog.

144 CHIEF JUSTICE Well, I am loath to gall a new-healed wound. Your day's service at Shrewsbury hath a little gilded over your night's exploit on Gad's Hill. You may
147 thank the unquiet time for your quiet o'erposting that action.

FALSTAFF My lord?

150 CHIEF JUSTICE But since all is well, keep it so. Wake not a sleeping wolf.

152 FALSTAFF To wake a wolf is as bad as smell a fox.

CHIEF JUSTICE What! You are as a candle, the better part burnt out.

155 FALSTAFF A wassail candle, my lord, all tallow. If I did
156 say of wax, my growth would approve the truth.

CHIEF JUSTICE There is not a white hair in your face but
158 should have his effect of gravity.

FALSTAFF His effect of gravy, gravy, gravy.

160 CHIEF JUSTICE You follow the young prince up and down like his ill angel.

162 FALSTAFF Not so, my lord. Your ill angel is light, but I
163 hope he that looks upon me will take me without weigh-
164 ing. And yet, in some respects, I grant, I cannot go. I

---

137 *means* financial resources   144 *gall* spur, irritate   147 *o'erposting* escape from the consequences of   152 *smell a fox* be suspicious   155 *wassail candle* large candle used at feasts; *tallow* animal fat   156 *wax* i.e., beeswax; *approve* prove   158 *effect* sign   162 *ill angel* (literally, a clipped coin)   163–64 *weighing* i.e., to determine value   164 *go* pass for currency

cannot tell. Virtue is of so little regard in these coster- 165
mongers' times that true valor is turned bearherd. Preg- 166
nancy is made a tapster, and hath his quick wit wasted in 167
giving reckonings. All the other gifts appertinent to 168
man, as the malice of this age shapes them, are not worth
a gooseberry. You that are old consider not the capacities 170
of us that are young; you do measure the heat of our liv-
ers with the bitterness of your galls. And we that are in 172
the vaward of our youth, I must confess, are wags too. 173

CHIEF JUSTICE   Do you set down your name in the scroll
of youth, that are written down old with all the characters of age? Have you not a moist eye? A dry hand? A
yellow cheek? A white beard? A decreasing leg? An in-
creasing belly? Is not your voice broken? Your wind
short? Your chin double? Your wit single? And every
part about you blasted with antiquity? And will you yet 180
call yourself young? Fie, fie, fie, Sir John! 181

FALSTAFF   My lord, I was born about three of the clock in
the afternoon, with a white head and something a 183
round belly. For my voice, I have lost it with halloing 184
and singing of anthems. To approve my youth further, I
will not. The truth is, I am only old in judgment and
understanding; and he that will caper with me for a 187
thousand marks, let him lend me the money, and have 188
at him! For the box of the ear that the prince gave you, 189
he gave it like a rude prince, and you took it like a sen- 190
sible lord. I have checked him for it, and the young lion
repents; marry, not in ashes and sackcloth, but in new
silk and old sack. 193

165–66 *costermonger's times* i.e., materialistic days   166 *bearherd* (a low oc-
cupation)   166–67 *Pregnancy* intellectual prowess   167 *tapster* bartender
168 *reckoning* bills   168 *appertinent* belonging   172 *galls* gallbladder, considered the source of ill-feeling   173 *vaward* vanguard, bloom   181 *Fie*
shame   183 *a of* a   184 *halloing* shouting to hounds (during hunting)
187 *caper* dance   188 *marks* coins worth two thirds of a pound (thirteen
shillings four pence)   189 *For* as for   193 *sack* a Spanish wine

CHIEF JUSTICE Well, God send the prince a better companion!

FALSTAFF God send the companion a better prince! I
cannot rid my hands of him.

CHIEF JUSTICE Well, the king hath severed you and Prince
Harry. I hear you are going with Lord John of Lancaster
200   against the archbishop and the Earl of Northumberland.

FALSTAFF Yea, I thank your pretty sweet wit for it. But
202   look you pray, all you that kiss my lady Peace at home,
that our armies join not in a hot day, for, by the Lord, I
take but two shirts out with me, and I mean not to sweat
extraordinarily. If it be a hot day, and I brandish any-
206   thing but a bottle, I would I might never spit white
again. There is not a dangerous action can peep out his
head but I am thrust upon it. Well, I cannot last ever. But
209   it was alway yet the trick of our English nation, if they
210   have a good thing, to make it too common. If ye will
needs say I am an old man, you should give me rest. I
would to God my name were not so terrible to the enemy
as it is. I were better to be eaten to death with a rust than
to be scoured to nothing with perpetual motion.

CHIEF JUSTICE Well, be honest, be honest, and God
bless your expedition!

FALSTAFF Will your lordship lend me a thousand pound
to furnish me forth?

CHIEF JUSTICE Not a penny, not a penny. You are too
220   impatient to bear crosses. Fare you well. Commend me
to my cousin Westmoreland.

        [Exeunt Chief Justice and Servant.]
222   FALSTAFF If I do, fillip me with a three-man beetle. A
man can no more separate age and covetousness than a
224   can part young limbs and lechery. But the gout galls the

---

202 *look you pray* be sure to pray   206 *spit white* spit clear – i.e., healthily or
thirstily   209 *trick* habit   220 *crosses* (1) trials, (2) coins stamped with a
cross   222 *fillip* strike; *three-man beetle* battering ram requiring three men to
lift it   224 *gout* a disease of overeating

one and the pox pinches the other, and so both the de-   225
grees prevent my curses. Boy!   226
PAGE   Sir?
FALSTAFF   What money is in my purse?
PAGE   Seven groats and two pence.
FALSTAFF   I can get no remedy against this consumption   230
of the purse. Borrowing only lingers and lingers it out,   231
but the disease is incurable. Go bear this letter to my
Lord of Lancaster, this to the prince, this to the Earl of
Westmoreland, and this to old Mistress Ursula, whom I
have weekly sworn to marry since I perceived the first
white hair of my chin. About it. You know where to   236
find me. *[Exit Page.]* A pox of this gout! Or a gout of
this pox! For the one or the other plays the rogue with
my great toe. 'Tis no matter if I do halt; I have the wars   239
for my color, and my pension shall seem the more rea-   240
sonable. A good wit will make use of anything. I will
turn diseases to commodity.   *[Exit.]*   242

*

∾ **I.3** *Enter the Archbishop, Thomas Mowbray [Earl
Marshal], the Lords Hastings and Bardolph.*

ARCHBISHOP
Thus have you heard our cause and known our means;
And, my honest noble friends, I pray you all,
Speak plainly your opinions of our hopes.
And first, lord marshal, what say you to it?
MOWBRAY
I well allow the occasion of our arms,   5
But gladly would be better satisfied   6

---

225 *pox* venereal disease   226 *prevent* anticipate   230 *consumption* wasting
disease   231 *lingers* delays   236 *About it* get a move on   239 *halt* limp
240 *color* excuse   242 *commodity* profit
   I.3 The palace of the Archbishop of York   5 *allow the occasion* admit the
need for   6–7 *satisfied / How* satisfied as to how

7   How in our means we should advance ourselves
To look with forehead bold and big enough
9   Upon the power and puissance of the king.

HASTINGS

10   Our present musters grow upon the file
To five-and-twenty thousand men of choice;
And our supplies live largely in the hope
Of great Northumberland, whose bosom burns
With an incensèd fire of injuries.

LORD BARDOLPH

The question then, Lord Hastings, standeth thus:
Whether our present five-and-twenty thousand
May hold up head without Northumberland?

HASTINGS

With him, we may.

LORD BARDOLPH   Yea, marry, there's the point.
But if without him we be thought too feeble,
20   My judgment is, we should not step too far
21   [Till we had his assistance by the hand.
22   For in a theme so bloody-faced as this,
Conjecture, expectation, and surmise
Of aids incertain should not be admitted.]

ARCHBISHOP

'Tis very true, Lord Bardolph, for indeed
It was young Hotspur's case at Shrewsbury.

LORD BARDOLPH

27   It was, my lord, who lined himself with hope,
28   Eating the air on promise of supply,
29   Flattering himself in project of a power
30   Much smaller than the smallest of his thoughts,
And so, with great imagination

---

7 *means* powers 9 *puissance* power (French) 10 *musters* enlistments; *file* roll 21 *by the hand* i.e., fast, close by 22 *theme* matter 27 *who* i.e., Hotspur; *lined* reinforced 28 *supply* reinforcement 29 *project* anticipation

Proper to madmen, led his powers to death   32
And winking leaped into destruction.   33
HASTINGS
But, by your leave, it never yet did hurt
To lay down likelihoods and forms of hope.   35
LORD BARDOLPH
[Yes, if this present quality of war,   36
Indeed the instant action, a cause on foot,
Lives so in hope as in an early spring
We see the appearing buds, which to prove fruit,
Hope gives not so much warrant as despair   40
That frosts will bite them. When we mean to build,
We first survey the plot, then draw the model.   42
And when we see the figure of the house,   43
Then must we rate the cost of the erection,   44
Which if we find outweighs ability,   45
What do we then but draw anew the model
In fewer offices, or at least desist   47
To build at all? Much more, in this great work,
Which is almost to pluck a kingdom down
And set another up, should we survey   50
The plot of situation and the model,   51
Consent upon a sure foundation,   52
Question surveyors, know our own estate,   53
How able such a work to undergo,
To weigh against his opposite. Or else]   55
We fortify in paper and in figures,   56
Using the names of men instead of men,

---

32 *powers* forces   **33** *winking* shutting his eyes   **35** *lay down* estimate   **36–41** *Yes . . . them* yes, it can do harm if we hope, just as in an early spring we see buds of which we have more despair than hope of their being nipped by frost than turning into fruit (text possibly corrupt)   **42** *model* plan   **43** *figure* design   **44** *rate* estimate   **45** *ability* power to pay   **47** *In fewer offices* with fewer rooms   **51** *plot of situation* i.e., lay of the land   **52** *Consent* agree   **53** *surveyors* architects; *estate* resources   **55** *his opposite* i.e., the king's side (?)   **56** *in* on

Like one that draws the model of a house
Beyond his power to build it, who, half through,
60 Gives o'er and leaves his part-created cost
A naked subject to the weeping clouds
And waste for churlish winter's tyranny.

HASTINGS
63 Grant that our hopes, yet likely of fair birth,
Should be still-born, and that we now possessed
65 The utmost man of expectation,
I think we are a body strong enough,
Even as we are, to equal with the king.

LORD BARDOLPH
What, is the king but five-and-twenty thousand?

HASTINGS
To us no more, nay, not so much, Lord Bardolph.
70 For his divisions, as the times do brawl,
71 Are in three heads: one power against the French,
72 And one against Glendower, perforce a third
Must take up us. So is the unfirm king
74 In three divided, and his coffers sound
With hollow poverty and emptiness.

ARCHBISHOP
76 That he should draw his several strengths together
And come against us in full puissance
Need not be dreaded.

HASTINGS   If he should do so,
[He leaves his back unarmed, the French and Welsh]
80 Baying him at the heels. Never fear that.

LORD BARDOLPH
81 Who is it like should lead his forces hither?

HASTINGS
The Duke of Lancaster and Westmoreland.
Against the Welsh, himself and Harry Monmouth.

---

60 *part-created cost* half-finished expense   63 *yet* still   65 *utmost . . . expectation* i.e., every anticipated man   71 *in three heads* divided in three   72 *perforce* of necessity   74 *sound* echo   76 *several* separate   81 *like* likely

But who is substituted 'gainst the French,   84
I have no certain notice.
[ARCHBISHOP   Let us on,
   And publish the occasion of our arms.   86
   The commonwealth is sick of their own choice;   87
   Their overgreedy love hath surfeited.   88
   An habitation giddy and unsure
   Hath he that buildeth on the vulgar heart.   90
   O thou fond many, with what loud applause   91
   Didst thou beat heaven with blessing Bolingbroke,   92
   Before he was what thou wouldst have him be!
   And being now trimmed in thine own desires,   94
   Thou, beastly feeder, art so full of him
   That thou provok'st thyself to cast him up.   96
   So, so, thou common dog, didst thou disgorge   97
   Thy glutton bosom of the royal Richard;
   And now thou wouldst eat thy dead vomit up,
   And howl'st to find it. What trust is in these times?   *100*
   They that when Richard lived would have him die
   Are now become enamored on his grave.
   Thou that threw'st dust upon his goodly head   103
   When through proud London he came sighing on
   After the admired heels of Bolingbroke
   Criest now, "O earth, yield us that king again,
   And take thou this!" O thoughts of men accursed!   107
   Past and to come seems best, things present worst.]
[MOWBRAY]
   Shall we go draw our numbers and set on?   109
HASTINGS
   We are time's subjects, and time bids be gone.   *[Exeunt.]*   *110*
                        *

---

84 *substituted* delegated to fight   **86** *publish* announce in public   **87** *choice* i.e., Henry IV   **88** *surfeited* i.e., glutted itself   **90** *vulgar* common, plebeian   **91** *fond many* foolish multitude   **92** *beat* assail (with prayers)   **94** *trimmed* dressed, furnished with   **96** *cast* vomit   **97** *disgorge* expel   **103** *Thou* i.e., the multitude   **107** *this* i.e., Henry IV   **109** *draw our numbers* assemble our forces

❧ **II.1** *Enter Hostess of the Tavern and an Officer or two [Fang and another, followed by Snare].*

1 HOSTESS   Master Fang, have you entered the action?
  FANG   It is entered.
3 HOSTESS   Where's your yeoman? Is't a lusty yeoman?
  Will a stand to't?
  FANG   *[To Officer]* Sirrah, where's Snare?
  HOSTESS   O Lord, ay! Good Master Snare.
  SNARE   Here, here.
  FANG   Snare, we must arrest Sir John Falstaff.
9 HOSTESS   Yea, good Master Snare, I have entered him
10 and all.
11 SNARE   It may chance cost some of us our lives, for he
  will stab.
13 HOSTESS   Alas the day! Take heed of him. He stabbed me
  in mine own house, and that most beastly. In good
  faith, he cares not what mischief he does, if his weapon
  be out. He will foin like any devil; he will spare neither
  man, woman, nor child.
18 FANG   If I can close with him, I care not for his thrust.
  HOSTESS   No, nor I neither. I'll be at your elbow.
20 FANG   An I but fist him once, and a come but within my
21 vice –
22 HOSTESS   I am undone by his going. I warrant you, he's
23 an infinitive thing upon my score. Good Master Fang,
24 hold him sure. Good Master Snare, let him not scape.
25 A comes continuantly to Pie Corner – saving your
26 manhoods – to buy a saddle; and he is indited to din-

II.1 Outside an Eastcheap tavern   1 *entered the action* initiated the lawsuit
3 *yeoman* sheriff's servant   9 *entered* brought a court action   11 *chance* per-
chance, perhaps   13 *stabbed me* (implying sexual intercourse, also with
"foin" and "thrust," ll. 16,18)   18 *close* grapple   20 *fist* (1) seize, (2) punch;
and a if he   21 *vice* grip   22 *undone* i.e., financially   23 *infinitive* i.e., infi-
nite   24 *sure* fast   25 *continuantly* i.e., continuously   26 *saddle* (1) horse
tack, (2) of mutton, (3) prostitute; *indited* i.e., invited

ner to the Lubber's Head in Lumbert Street, to Master 27
Smooth's the silkman. I pray you, since my exion is en- 28
tered and my case so openly known to the world, let 29
him be brought in to his answer. A hundred mark is a 30
long one for a poor lone woman to bear, and I have
borne, and borne, and borne, and have been fubbed 32
off, and fubbed off, and fubbed off, from this day to
that day, that it is a shame to be thought on. There is
no honesty in such dealing, unless a woman should be
made an ass and a beast, to bear every knave's wrong.
Yonder he comes, and that arrant malmsey-nose knave, 37
Bardolph, with him. Do your offices, do your offices. 38
Master Fang and Master Snare, do me, do me, do me
your offices. 40

 Enter Sir John [Falstaff] and Bardolph, and the Boy
 [Page].

FALSTAFF How now! Whose mare's dead? What's the 41
matter?

FANG Sir John, I arrest you at the suit of Mistress
Quickly.

FALSTAFF Away, varlets! Draw, Bardolph. Cut me off the 45
villain's head. Throw the quean in the channel. 46

HOSTESS Throw me in the channel! I'll throw thee in the
channel. Wilt thou? Wilt thou? Thou bastardly rogue!
Murder, murder! Ah, thou honeysuckle villain! Wilt 49
thou kill God's officers and the king's? Ah, thou honey- 50
seed rogue! Thou art a honeyseed, a man-queller, and a 51
woman-queller. 52

---

27 *Lubber's Head* i.e., Leopard's Head (a shop sign) 28 *exion* action 29
case legal action; also slang for female sexual organs 30 *mark* thirteen
shillings four pence 32 *fubbed* fobbed, put 37 *malmsey-nose* red-nosed
from imbibing wine 38 *Do your offices* execute your business (with innu-
endo of performing sexual service) 41 *Whose mare's dead* i.e., what's all the
fuss about 45 *varlets* scoundrels; *Draw* i.e., your sword 46 *quean* whore;
channel gutter 49 *honeysuckle* i.e., homicidal 50–51 *honeyseed* i.e., homi-
cide 51 *man-queller* i.e., man-killer 52 *woman-queller* (1) woman-killer,
(2) seducer

FALSTAFF   Keep them off, Bardolph.

FANG   A rescue! A rescue!

HOSTESS   Good people, bring a rescue or two. Thou wo't,
wo't thou? Thou wo't, wo't ta? Do, do, thou rogue! Do,
57   thou hempseed!

58   PAGE   Away, you scullion! You rampallian! You fustilar-
59   ian! I'll tickle your catastrophe.

Enter Lord Chief Justice and his Men.

CHIEF JUSTICE

60   What is the matter? Keep the peace here, ho!

HOSTESS   Good my lord, be good to me. I beseech you,
62   stand to me.

CHIEF JUSTICE

How now, Sir John! What are you brawling here?
Doth this become your place, your time and business?
You should have been well on your way to York.
Stand from him, fellow. Wherefore hang'st upon him?

HOSTESS   O my most worshipful lord, an't please your
grace, I am a poor widow of Eastcheap, and he is ar-
rested at my suit.

70   CHIEF JUSTICE   For what sum?

HOSTESS   It is more than for some, my lord; it is for all,
all I have. He hath eaten me out of house and home; he
hath put all my substance into that fat belly of his. But
I will have some of it out again, or I will ride thee o'
75   nights like the mare.

76   FALSTAFF   I think I am as like to ride the mare, if I have
any vantage of ground to get up.

CHIEF JUSTICE   How comes this, Sir John? Fie! What
man of good temper would endure this tempest of ex-
80   clamation? Are you not ashamed to enforce a poor
widow to so rough a course to come by her own?

---

57 *hempseed* (hemp refers to the hangman's rope)   58 *scullion* kitchen
wench; *rampallian* scoundrel   58–59 *fustilarian* fat, blowzy woman, floozy
59 *catastrophe* i.e., backside   62 *stand to* (1) help, (2) service sexually   75
mare nightmare   76 *ride the mare* (Falstaff sexualizes the phrase, as he does
"get up" in the following line)

FALSTAFF   What is the gross sum that I owe thee?

HOSTESS   Marry, if thou wert an honest man, thyself and
the money too. Thou didst swear to me upon a parcel-   84
gilt goblet, sitting in my Dolphin chamber, at the round   85
table, by a sea-coal fire, upon Wednesday in Wheeson   86
week, when the prince broke thy head for liking his fa-   87
ther to a singing-man of Windsor, thou didst swear to   88
me then, as I was washing thy wound, to marry me and
make me my lady thy wife. Canst thou deny it? Did not   90
goodwife Keech, the butcher's wife, come in then and
call me gossip Quickly? Coming in to borrow a mess of   92
vinegar, telling us she had a good dish of prawns, where- 93
by thou didst desire to eat some, whereby I told thee
they were ill for a green wound? And didst thou not,   95
when she was gone down stairs, desire me to be no more
so familiarity with such poor people, saying that ere   97
long they should call me madam? And didst thou not
kiss me and bid me fetch thee thirty shillings? I put thee
now to thy book-oath. Deny it, if thou canst.   100

FALSTAFF   My lord, this is a poor mad soul, and she says
up and down the town that her eldest son is like you.
She hath been in good case, and the truth is, poverty   103
hath distracted her. But for these foolish officers, I be- 104
seech you I may have redress against them.

CHIEF JUSTICE   Sir John, Sir John, I am well acquainted
with your manner of wrenching the true cause the false
way. It is not a confident brow, nor the throng of words 108
that come with such more than impudent sauciness
from you, can thrust me from a level consideration.   110

84–85 *parcel-gilt* partly gilded   85 *Dolphin chamber* (room in her tavern)
86 *sea-coal* mineral coal (not charcoal) brought by sea; *Wheeson* Whitsun
(Pentecost)   87 *liking* comparing   88 *singing-man* choral singer   92 *gossip*
(term for female friend); *mess* small amount   93 *prawns* shrimp   95 *green*
raw, new   97 *familiarity* familiar, intimate   100 *book-oath* i.e., sworn on
the Bible   103 *in good case* prosperous (with sexual suggestion)   104 *distracted her* driven her mad   108 *confident brow* good front   110 *level* judi-
cious, unbiased

You have, as it appears to me, practiced upon the easy-yielding spirit of this woman, and made her serve your uses both in purse and in person.

HOSTESS   Yea, in truth, my lord.

CHIEF JUSTICE   Pray thee, peace. Pay her the debt you owe her and unpay the villainy you have done with her. The one you may do with sterling money, and the other with current repentance.

FALSTAFF   My lord, I will not undergo this sneap without reply. You call honorable boldness impudent sauciness. If a man will make curtsy and say nothing, he is virtuous. No, my lord, my humble duty remembered, I will not be your suitor. I say to you, I do desire deliverance from these officers, being upon hasty employment in the king's affairs.

CHIEF JUSTICE   You speak as having power to do wrong. But answer in the effect of your reputation, and satisfy the poor woman.

FALSTAFF   Come hither, hostess.

Enter a Messenger [Gower].

CHIEF JUSTICE   Now, Master Gower, what news?

GOWER
The king, my lord, and Harry Prince of Wales
Are near at hand. The rest the paper tells.

FALSTAFF   As I am a gentleman.

HOSTESS   Faith, you said so before.

FALSTAFF   As I am a gentleman. Come, no more words of it.

HOSTESS   By this heavenly ground I tread on, I must be fain to pawn both my plate and the tapestry of my dining-chambers.

---

118 *current* lawful (with allusion to currency)   119 *sneap* rebuke, correction
127 *in . . . reputation* in a manner suited to your reputation (as a knight)
138 *fain* obliged; *plate* pewter

FALSTAFF   Glasses, glasses, is the only drinking. And for   140
thy walls, a pretty slight drollery, or the story of the   141
Prodigal, or the German hunting in water-work, is   142
worth a thousand of these bed-hangings and these fly-
bitten tapestries. Let it be ten pound, if thou canst.
Come, an 'twere not for thy humors, there's not a better   145
wench in England. Go, wash thy face, and draw the ac-   146
tion. Come, thou must not be in this humor with me.
Dost not know me? Come, come, I know thou wast set
on to this.

HOSTESS   Pray thee, Sir John, let it be but twenty nobles.   150
I' faith, I am loath to pawn my plate, so God save me, la!   151

FALSTAFF   Let it alone; I'll make other shift. You'll be a   152
fool still.

HOSTESS   Well, you shall have it, though I pawn my
gown. I hope you'll come to supper. You'll pay me all
together?

FALSTAFF   Will I live? [To Bardolph] Go, with her, with
her. Hook on, hook on.   158

HOSTESS   Will you have Doll Tearsheet meet you at
supper?   160

FALSTAFF   No more words. Let's have her.
    Exeunt Hostess and Sergeant [Fang, Bardolph, and
    others].

CHIEF JUSTICE   I have heard better news.

FALSTAFF   What's the news, my lord?

CHIEF JUSTICE   Where lay the king last night?

GOWER   At Basingstoke, my lord.

FALSTAFF   I hope, my lord, all's well. What is the news,
my lord?

CHIEF JUSTICE   Come all his forces back?

---

140 *the only* the most fashionable   141 *drollery* comic picture   142 *Prodigal* Bible story of the prodigal son; *German hunting* Dutch or German hunting scene   145 *humors* moods   146 *draw* withdraw   150 *nobles* coins
worth six shillings eight pence (not the ten pounds he requested)   151 *loath*
reluctant   152 *shift* arrangements   158 *Hook on* stay close (to her)

GOWER
   No. Fifteen hundred foot, five hundred horse,
170 Are marched up to my lord of Lancaster,
   Against Northumberland and the archbishop.
FALSTAFF
   Comes the king back from Wales, my noble lord?
CHIEF JUSTICE
   You shall have letters of me presently.
   Come, go along with me, good Master Gower.
FALSTAFF   My lord!
CHIEF JUSTICE   What's the matter?
177 FALSTAFF   Master Gower, shall I entreat you with me to
   dinner?
GOWER   I must wait upon my good lord here, I thank
180 you, good Sir John.
181 CHIEF JUSTICE   Sir John, you loiter here too long, being
182 you are to take soldiers up in counties as you go.
FALSTAFF   Will you sup with me, Master Gower?
CHIEF JUSTICE   What foolish master taught you these
   manners, Sir John?
FALSTAFF   Master Gower, if they become me not, he was
187 a fool that taught them me. This is the right fencing
188 grace, my lord – tap for tap, and so part fair.
189 CHIEF JUSTICE   Now the Lord lighten thee! Thou art a
190 great fool.   *[Exeunt.]*

*

∾ **II.2** *Enter the Prince [Henry], and Poins, with others.*

PRINCE   Before God, I am exceeding weary.
POINS   Is't come to that? I had thought weariness durst
3 not have attached one of so high blood.

---

177 *entreat* invite   181 *being* being as   182 *take soldiers* conscript   187–
88 *fencing grace* (Falstaff pays the Chief Justice back in kind for ignoring his
earlier questions)   188 *fair* even   189 *lighten* enlighten
   II.2 London, Prince Henry's quarters   3 *attached* seized, attended

PRINCE   Faith, it does me, though it discolors the com-   4
plexion of my greatness to acknowledge it. Doth it not
show vilely in me to desire small beer?   6

POINS   Why, a prince should not be so loosely studied as   7
to remember so weak a composition.   8

PRINCE   Belike, then, my appetite was not princely got,
for, by my troth, I do now remember the poor creature,   10
small beer. But indeed these humble considerations
make me out of love with my greatness. What a disgrace is it to me to remember thy name! Or to know
thy face tomorrow! Or to take note how many pair of
silk stockings thou hast, viz. these, and those that were
thy peach-colored ones! Or to bear the inventory of thy   16
shirts, as, one for superfluity, and another for use! But   17
that the tennis-court-keeper knows better than I; for it
is a low ebb of linen with thee when thou keepest not
racket there, as thou hast not done a great while, be-   20
cause the rest of thy low countries have made a shift to   21
eat up thy holland. And God knows whether those that   22
bawl out the ruins of thy linen shall inherit his king-   23
dom. But the midwives say the children are not in the
fault, whereupon the world increases, and kindreds are   25
mightily strengthened.

POINS   How ill it follows, after you have labored so hard,   27
you should talk so idly! Tell me, how many good young
princes would do so, their fathers being so sick as yours
at this time is?   30

PRINCE   Shall I tell thee one thing, Poins?

4–5 *discolors . . . greatness* makes the face of my greatness blush   6 *small*
weak, inferior   7 *so loosely studied* so careless a student   8 *composition* (1)
weak beer, (2) details   16 *bear* bear in mind   17 *superfluity* extra   17–20
But . . . while but the keeper of the tennis court knows that you are short on
shirts, as you've not been seen there lately   21 *low countries* brothels (with a
pun on "Netherlands"); *made a shift* contrived   22 *eat up* spend; *holland*
linen   22–23 *those . . . linen* (Poins's bastards, clothed in his shirts recycled
as swaddling clothes)   23 *bawl out* (1) cry out, (2) declare   25 *kindreds* families, populations   27 *labored so hard* i.e., in the civil wars, or in search of a
play on words

POINS   Yes, faith, and let it be an excellent good thing.

PRINCE   It shall serve among wits of no higher breeding than thine.

35 POINS   Go to. I stand the push of your one thing that you will tell.

37 PRINCE   Marry, I tell thee, it is not meet that I should be sad, now my father is sick. Albeit I could tell to thee, as to one it pleases me, for fault of a better, to call my 40 friend, I could be sad, and sad indeed too.

41 POINS   Very hardly upon such a subject.

42 PRINCE   By this hand, thou thinkest me as far in the 43 devil's book as thou and Falstaff for obduracy and per-44 sistency. Let the end try the man. But I tell thee, my heart bleeds inwardly that my father is so sick. And keeping such vile company as thou art hath in reason 47 taken from me all ostentation of sorrow.

POINS   The reason?

PRINCE   What wouldst thou think of me if I should 50 weep?

POINS   I would think thee a most princely hypocrite.

PRINCE   It would be every man's thought, and thou art a blessed fellow to think as every man thinks. Never a 54 man's thought in the world keeps the roadway better than thine. Every man would think me an hypocrite in-56 deed. And what accites your most worshipful thought to think so?

58 POINS   Why, because you have been so lewd and so 59 much engraffed to Falstaff.

60 PRINCE   And to thee.

61 POINS   By this light, I am well spoke on; I can hear it 62 with mine own ears. The worst that they can say of me

---

35 *stand the push* withstand the thrust   37 *meet* suitable   41 *Very hardly* with great difficulty   42–43 *as far . . . book* as wicked   43 *obduracy* hardened sinning   44 *the end* (a reference to Hal's plan to play the prodigal)   47 *ostentation* outward display   54 *keeps . . . better* is so predictably common   56 *accites* prompts   58 *lewd* base, common   59 *engraffed* attached   61 *on* of   62 *mine own ears* i.e., to my face

is that I am a second brother and that I am a proper fel-   63
low of my hands, and those two things I confess I cannot help. By the mass, here comes Bardolph.

Enter Bardolph and Boy [Page].

PRINCE   And the boy that I gave Falstaff. A had him from   66
me Christian, and look if the fat villain have not transformed him ape.   68

BARDOLPH   God save your grace!

PRINCE   And yours, most noble Bardolph!   70

POINS   Come, you virtuous ass, you bashful fool, must
you be blushing? Wherefore blush you now? What a   72
maidenly man-at-arms are you become! Is't such a matter to get a pottle-pot's maidenhead?   74

PAGE   A calls me e'en now, my lord, through a red lattice,   75
and I could discern no part of his face from the window. At last I spied his eyes, and methought he had
made two holes in the ale-wife's new petticoat and so   78
peeped through.

PRINCE   Has not the boy profited?   80

BARDOLPH   Away, you whoreson upright rabbit, away!

PAGE   Away, you rascally Althaea's dream, away!   82

PRINCE   Instruct us, boy. What dream, boy?

PAGE   Marry, my lord, Althaea dreamed she was delivered of a firebrand, and therefore I call him her dream.

PRINCE   A crown's worth of good interpretation. There   86
'tis, boy.

POINS   O, that this good blossom could be kept from   88
cankers! Well, there is sixpence to preserve thee.   89

---

63 *second brother* i.e., not in line to inherit as firstborn son   **63–64** *proper . . . hands* good fighter   **66** *A* he (meaning Falstaff)   **68** *him ape* him into an ape   **72** *blushing* (a derisive comment on Bardolph's red – from drinking – face)   **74** *pottle-pot* two-quart tankard   **75** *red lattice* (that of a tavern window)   **78** *new petticoat* (red, presumably)   **80** *profited* learned well   **82** *Althaea* (in Ovid's *Heroides,* she dreamt that a brand placed on the fire by the Fates remained unburnt; confused here with Hecuba, who, while pregnant with Paris, dreamt she was delivered of a firebrand that would destroy Troy)   **86** *crown* five shillings   **88** *good blossom* i.e., the page   **89** *cankers* canker worms

90 BARDOLPH An you do not make him hanged among
you, the gallows shall have wrong.
PRINCE And how doth thy master, Bardolph?
BARDOLPH Well, my lord. He heard of your grace's coming to town. There's a letter for you.
95 POINS Delivered with good respect. And how doth the
96 martlemas, your master?
BARDOLPH In bodily health, sir.
POINS Marry, the immortal part needs a physician, but
99 that moves not him. Though that be sick, it dies not.
100 PRINCE I do allow this wen to be as familiar with me as
my dog, and he holds his place, for look you how he
writes.
POINS *[Reads.]* "John Falstaff, knight" – every man must
know that, as oft as he has occasion to name himself.
Even like those that are kin to the king, for they never
prick their finger but they say, "There's some of the
king's blood spilt." "How comes that?" says he that
108 takes upon him not to conceive. The answer is as ready
as a borrower's cap, "I am the king's poor cousin, sir."
110 PRINCE Nay, they will be kin to us, or they will fetch it
from Japhet. But to the letter. *[Reads.]* "Sir John Falstaff, knight, to the son of the king, nearest his father,
Harry Prince of Wales, greeting."
114 POINS Why, this is a certificate.
PRINCE Peace! *[Reads.]* "I will imitate the honorable Ro-
mans in brevity."
POINS He sure means brevity in breath, short-winded.
[PRINCE *Reads.*] "I commend me to thee, I commend
thee, and I leave thee. Be not too familiar with Poins,
120 for he misuses thy favors so much that he swears thou

---

95 *good respect* due ceremony (spoken ironically) **96** *martlemas* beef cattle
fattened in anticipation of Martlemas day feast, November 11 **99** *that* i.e.,
Falstaff's soul **100** *wen* tumor **108** *conceive* understand **110–11**
fetch . . . Japhet trace their ancestry to Noah's son Japhet (Genesis 10:2–5),
father of all Europeans **114** *certificate* legal document (a license issued from
sovereign to subject) **120** *misuses thy favors* abuses thy friendship

art to marry his sister Nell. Repent at idle times as thou
mayest, and so farewell.

"Thine, by yea and no, which is as much as to say, as   123
thou usest him, JACK FALSTAFF with my familiars,   124
JOHN with my brothers and sisters, and SIR JOHN
with all Europe."

POINS   My lord, I'll steep this letter in sack and make
him eat it.

PRINCE   That's to make him eat twenty of his words. But
do you use me thus, Ned? Must I marry your sister?   130

POINS   God send the wench no worse fortune! But I
never said so.

PRINCE   Well, thus we play the fools with the time, and
the spirits of the wise sit in the clouds and mock us. Is
your master here in London?

BARDOLPH   Yea, my lord.

PRINCE   Where sups he? Doth the old boar feed in the
old frank?   138

BARDOLPH   At the old place, my lord, in Eastcheap.

PRINCE   What company?   140

PAGE   Ephesians, my lord, of the old church.   141

PRINCE   Sup any women with him?

PAGE   None, my lord, but old Mistress Quickly and Mistress Doll Tearsheet.

PRINCE   What pagan may that be?   145

PAGE   A proper gentlewoman, sir, and a kinswoman of
my master's.

PRINCE   Even such kin as the parish heifers are to the
town bull. Shall we steal upon them, Ned, at supper?

POINS   I am your shadow, my lord; I'll follow you.   150

PRINCE   Sirrah, you boy, and Bardolph, no word to your
master that I am yet come to town. There's for your
silence.

---

123 *by yea and no* (a parodic Puritan – hence insipid – oath)   124 *familiars*
intimates   138 *frank* pig sty   140 *What* i.e., in whose   141 *Ephesians . . .
church* good fellows of the usual gang   145 *pagan* harlot, strumpet

BARDOLPH   I have no tongue, sir.

PAGE   And for mine, sir, I will govern it.

PRINCE   Fare you well; go. *[Exeunt Bardolph and Page.]*

157   This Doll Tearsheet should be some road.

POINS   I warrant you, as common as the way between
Saint Alban's and London.

160   PRINCE   How might we see Falstaff bestow himself
tonight in his true colors, and not ourselves be seen?

162   POINS   Put on two leathern jerkins and aprons, and wait
163   upon him at his table as drawers.

PRINCE   From a God to a bull? A heavy descension! It
165   was Jove's case. From a prince to a prentice? A low
transformation! That shall be mine, for in everything
167   the purpose must weigh with the folly. Follow me,
Ned.

Exeunt.

*

∿ **II.3** *Enter Northumberland, his Wife [Lady
Northumberland], and the Wife to Harry Percy [Lady
Percy].*

NORTHUMBERLAND

1   I pray thee, loving wife, and gentle daughter,
2   Give even way unto my rough affairs.
Put not you on the visage of the times
And be like them to Percy troublesome.

LADY NORTHUMBERLAND

I have given over, I will speak no more.
Do what you will, your wisdom be your guide.

---

157 *road* i.e., whore, well traveled   160–61 *bestow . . . colors* behave in his
usual way   162 *jerkins* jackets   163 *drawers* tavern waiters   165 *Jove's case*
(Jove transformed himself into a bull in order to woo Europa, who was tending her father's cows); *prentice* apprentice   167 *weigh with* suit

II.3 Northumberland's castle   1 *daughter* i.e., daughter-in-law   2 *even
way* free scope

NORTHUMBERLAND
   Alas, sweet wife, my honor is at pawn,
   And, but my going, nothing can redeem it.   8
LADY PERCY
   O yet, for God's sake, go not to these wars!
   The time was, father, that you broke your word,   *10*
   When you were more endeared to it than now,   11
   When your own Percy, when my heart's dear Harry,
   Threw many a northward look to see his father
   Bring up his powers, but he did long in vain.   14
   Who then persuaded you to stay at home?
   There were two honors lost, yours and your son's.
   For yours, the God of heaven brighten it!   17
   For his, it stuck upon him as the sun
   In the gray vault of heaven, and by his light   *19*
   Did all the chivalry of England move   *20*
   To do brave acts. He was indeed the glass   21
   Wherein the noble youth did dress themselves.
   [He had no legs that practiced not his gait;
   And speaking thick, which nature made his blemish,   24
   Became the accents of the valiant,
   For those that could speak low and tardily
   Would turn their own perfection to abuse,
   To seem like him. So that in speech, in gait,
   In diet, in affections of delight,   29
   In military rules, humors of blood,   30
   He was the mark and glass, copy and book,
   That fashioned others. And him – O wondrous him!
   O miracle of men! – him did you leave,
   Second to none, unseconded by you,   34
   To look upon the hideous god of war
   In disadvantage, to abide a field   36

---

8 *but* except for **11** *endeared* committed **14** *in vain* (Northumberland failed to appear in support of Hotspur at Shrewsbury) **17** *For* as for **19** *gray* sky-blue **21** *glass* mirror **24** *thick* fast **29** *affections of delight* recreations **30** *humors of blood* temperament **34** *unseconded* left without reinforcements **36** *In* at a

Where nothing but the sound of Hotspur's name
38   Did seem defensible. So you left him.
        Never, O never, do his ghost the wrong
40   To hold your honor more precise and nice
        With others than with him! Let them alone.
        The marshal and the archbishop are strong.
        Had my sweet Harry had but half their numbers,
        Today might I, hanging on Hotspur's neck,
45   Have talked of Monmouth's grave.]
NORTHUMBERLAND   Beshrew your heart,
        Fair daughter, you do draw my spirits from me
47   With new lamenting ancient oversights.
        But I must go and meet with danger there,
        Or it will seek me in another place
50   And find me worse provided.
LADY NORTHUMBERLAND   O, fly to Scotland,
        Till that the nobles and the armèd commons
52   Have of their puissance made a little taste.
LADY PERCY
53   If they get ground and vantage of the king,
        Then join you with them, like a rib of steel,
        To make strength stronger. But, for all our loves,
        First let them try themselves. So did your son;
57   He was so suffered. So came I a widow,
        And never shall have length of life enough
59   To rain upon remembrance with mine eyes,
60   That it may grow and sprout as high as heaven,
61   For recordation to my noble husband.
NORTHUMBERLAND
        Come, come, go in with me. 'Tis with my mind
        As with the tide swelled up unto his height,

---

38 *defensible* capable of defense   40 *precise and nice* carefully   45 *Monmouth's* i.e., Prince Hal's; *Beshrew your heart* (a reproachful oath)   47 *new* freshly   52 *made . . . taste* been tried   53 *vantage* power over   57 *suffered* allowed (to fight unreinforced); *came* became   59 *rain* weep   61 *recordation* memorial

That makes a still-stand, running neither way.
Fain would I go to meet the archbishop,   65
But many thousand reasons hold me back.
I will resolve for Scotland. There am I,
Till time and vantage crave my company.   *Exeunt.*   68

*

∾ **II.4** *Enter a Drawer or two [Francis and a second].*

FRANCIS   What the devil hast thou brought there? Apple-   1
johns? Thou knowest Sir John cannot endure an apple-
john.
SECOND DRAWER   Mass, thou sayest true. The prince
once set a dish of apple-johns before him, and told him
there were five more Sir Johns, and, putting off his hat,   6
said, "I will now take my leave of these six dry, round,
old, withered knights." It angered him to the heart. But
he hath forgot that.
FRANCIS   Why, then, cover, and set them down. And see   10
if thou canst find out Sneak's noise; Mistress Tearsheet   11
would fain hear some music. Dispatch. The room
where they supped is too hot; they'll come in straight.
   Enter Will [a third Drawer].
THIRD DRAWER   Sirrah, here will be the prince and Master Poins anon, and they will put on two of our jerkins
and aprons, and Sir John must not know of it. Bardolph hath brought word.   *[Exit.]*
FRANCIS   By the mass, here will be old Utis. It will be an   18
excellent stratagem.
SECOND DRAWER   I'll see if I can find out Sneak.   *Exit.*   20

---

65 *Fain* eagerly   68 *vantage* advantage, occasion
   II.4 An Eastcheap tavern   1–2 *Apple-johns* apples eaten when shriveled
and dried   6 *putting off* taking off   10 *cover* lay the tablecloth   11 *noise*
band   18 *old Utis* high jinks (Utis = a long celebration, literally the eighth
day of a festival)

*Enter Mistress Quickly [the Hostess] and Doll
Tearsheet.*

HOSTESS   I' faith, sweetheart, methinks now you are in
22   an excellent good temperality. Your pulsidge beats as
extraordinarily as heart would desire, and your color, I
warrant you, is as red as any rose, in good truth, la! But,
25   i' faith, you have drunk too much canaries, and that's a
26   marvellous searching wine, and it perfumes the blood
ere one can say, "What's this?" How do you now?

DOLL   Better than I was. Hem!

HOSTESS   Why, that's well said. A good heart's worth
30   gold. Lo, here comes Sir John.

Enter Sir John [Falstaff].

31   FALSTAFF   *[Sings.]* "When Arthur first in court" – Empty
32   the jordan. *[Exit Francis.]* – *[Sings.]* "And was a worthy
king." – How now, Mistress Doll!

34   HOSTESS   Sick of a calm, yea, good faith.

35   FALSTAFF   So is all her sect. An they be once in a calm,
they are sick.

37   DOLL   A pox damn you, you muddy rascal, is that all the
comfort you give me?

39   FALSTAFF   You make fat rascals, Mistress Doll.

40   DOLL   I make them! Gluttony and diseases make them; I
make them not.

FALSTAFF   If the cook help to make the gluttony, you
43   help to make the diseases, Doll. We catch of you, Doll,
we catch of you. Grant that, my poor virtue, grant that.

45   DOLL   Yea, joy, our chains and our jewels.

---

22 *temperality* i.e., temper; *pulsidge* i.e., pulse   25 *canaries* sweet wine from
the Canary Islands   26 *searching* potent   31 *When . . . court* (a line from
the ballad "Sir Lancelot du Lac")   32 *jordan* chamber pot   34 *calm* i.e.,
qualm   35 *sect* (1) sex, (2) company of prostitutes; *in a calm* not plying their
trade   37 *muddy rascal* sluggish deer   39 *fat* swollen (with sexual suggestion: with an erection, or from venereal disease, thought to create obesity)
43 *diseases* i.e., venereal diseases   45 *Yea . . . jewels* yes, you catch (take) our
jewelry

FALSTAFF   "Your brooches, pearls, and ouches." For to   46
serve bravely is to come halting off, you know. To come   47
off the breach with his pike bent bravely, and to surgery
bravely; to venture upon the charged chambers   49
bravely –   50

DOLL   Hang yourself, you muddy conger, hang yourself!   51

HOSTESS   By my troth, this is the old fashion. You two   52
never meet but you fall to some discord. You are both, i'
good truth, as rheumatic as two dry toasts; you cannot   54
one bear with another's confirmities. What the good-   55
year! [To Doll] One must bear, and that must be you.   56
You are the weaker vessel, as they say, the emptier vessel.

DOLL   Can a weak empty vessel bear such a huge full
hogshead? There's a whole merchant's venture of Bor-   59
deaux stuff in him; you have not seen a hulk better   60
stuffed in the hold. Come, I'll be friends with thee,
Jack. Thou art going to the wars, and whether I shall
ever see thee again or no, there is nobody cares.

    Enter Drawer [Francis].

FRANCIS   Sir, Ancient Pistol's below and would speak   64
with you.

DOLL   Hang him, swaggering rascal! Let him not come   66
hither. It is the foul-mouth'st rogue in England.

HOSTESS   If he swagger, let him not come here. No, by
my faith. I must live among my neighbors, I'll no swag-   69
gerers. I am in good name and fame with the very best.   70
Shut the door, there comes no swaggerers here. I have
not lived all this while to have swaggering now. Shut
the door, I pray you.

---

46 Your . . . ouches (another phrase from a ballad); ouches jewels   47 serve
i.e., sexually; halting limping   49 charged chambers (1) small cannon, (2)
penis   51 conger eel   52 old fashion habit   54 rheumatic splenetic; toasts
(which grate upon each other)   55 conformities i.e., infirmities   55–56
What the good-year what the devil   56 bear (1) forebear, (2) bear children,
(3) bear the weight of a lover   59 venture shipload   60 stuff wine   64 Ancient ensign, lieutenant   66 swaggering hectoring   69 I'll no I'll have no

FALSTAFF Dost thou hear, hostess?

HOSTESS Pray ye, pacify yourself, Sir John. There comes no swaggerers here.

FALSTAFF Dost thou hear? It is mine ancient.

78 HOSTESS Tilly-fally, Sir John, ne'er tell me. Your ancient swaggerer comes not in my doors. I was before Master
80 Tisick, the debuty, t' other day, and, as he said to me, 'twas no longer ago than Wednesday last, "I' good faith, neighbor Quickly," says he – Master Dumbe, our min-
83 ister, was by then – "neighbor Quickly," says he, "re-
84 ceive those that are civil, for," said he, "you are in an ill
85 name." Now a said so, I can tell whereupon. "For," says he, "you are an honest woman, and well thought on; therefore take heed what guests you receive. Receive,"
88 says he, "no swaggering companions." There comes none here. You would bless you to hear what he said.
90 No, I'll no swaggerers.

91 FALSTAFF He's no swaggerer, hostess; a tame cheater, i' faith; you may stroke him as gently as a puppy grey-
93 hound. He'll not swagger with a Barbary hen, if her feathers turn back in any show of resistance. Call him up, drawer.   *[Exit Francis.]*

HOSTESS Cheater, call you him? I will bar no honest man my house, nor no cheater. But I do not love swag-gering, by my troth; I am the worse when one says swagger. Feel, masters, how I shake, look you, I warrant
100 you.

DOLL So you do, hostess.

102 HOSTESS Do I? Yea, in very truth, do I, an 'twere an aspen leaf. I cannot abide swaggerers.
     Enter Ancient Pistol, [Bardolph,] and Bardolph's Boy [Page].

---

78 *Tilly-fally* phooey, nonsense 80 *debuty* i.e., deputy 83 *by* nearby
84–85 *in . . . name* have a bad reputation 85 *whereupon* why 88 *compan-ions* ruffians 91 *tame cheater* decoy in a card game 93 *Barbary* hen guinea hen (slang for prostitute) 102 *an 'twere* as if I were

PISTOL   God save you, Sir John!

FALSTAFF   Welcome, Ancient Pistol. Here, Pistol, I charge you with a cup of sack. Do you discharge upon   106
mine hostess.

PISTOL   I will discharge upon her, Sir John, with two bullets.   109

FALSTAFF   She is pistol-proof, sir; you shall hardly offend   110
her.

HOSTESS   Come, I'll drink no proofs nor no bullets. I'll drink no more than will do me good, for no man's pleasure, I.

PISTOL   Then to you, Mistress Dorothy; I will charge you.

DOLL   Charge me! I scorn you, scurvy companion. What! You poor, base, rascally, cheating, lack-linen   118
mate! Away, you moldy rogue, away! I am meat for   119
your master.   120

PISTOL   I know you, Mistress Dorothy.

DOLL   Away, you cut-purse rascal! You filthy bung, away!   122
By this wine, I'll thrust my knife in your moldy chaps,   123
an you play the saucy cuttle with me. Away, you bottle-   124
ale rascal! You basket-hilt stale juggler, you! Since when,   125
I pray you, sir? God's light, with two points on your   126
shoulder? Much!   127

PISTOL   God let me not live but I will murder your ruff   128
for this.

<hr />

106 *charge* toast; *discharge upon* drink to (with sexual suggestion, and play upon the name "Pistol") 109 *bullets* i.e., testicles 110 *pistol-proof* past childbearing age (?); *offend* wound 118 *lack-linen* shirtless 119 *meat* (with sexual suggestion, and play upon "meet," fit for, and "mate") 122 *cut-purse* thief (with sexual suggestion, "purse" being slang for vagina as well as scrotum); *bung* (1) pickpocket, (2) plug for a hole 123 *chaps* cheeks 124 *cuttle* cutthroat 125 *basket-hilt* a handle for a practice sword (Doll accuses Pistol of not wearing – or having – the real thing); *juggler* impostor 126 *two points* laces for securing armor to the shoulder 127 *Much* (a deri-sive exclamation) 128 *murder your ruff* tear your starched and pleated col-lar (prostitutes were partial to large ones)

130 FALSTAFF   No more, Pistol; I would not have you go off
here. Discharge yourself of our company, Pistol.

HOSTESS   No, good Captain Pistol, not here, sweet captain.

DOLL   Captain! Thou abominable damned cheater, art
thou not ashamed to be called captain? An captains
136 were of my mind, they would truncheon you out for
taking their names upon you before you have earned
them. You a captain! You slave, for what? For tearing a
poor whore's ruff in a bawdy-house? He a captain!
140 Hang him, rogue! He lives upon moldy stewed prunes
and dried cakes. A captain! God's light, these villains
142 will make the word as odious as the word "occupy,"
143 which was an excellent good word before it was ill
sorted. Therefore captains had need look to't.

BARDOLPH   Pray thee, go down, good ancient.

FALSTAFF   Hark thee hither, Mistress Doll.

PISTOL   Not I. I tell thee what, Corporal Bardolph, I
148 could tear her. I'll be revenged of her.

PAGE   Pray thee, go down.

150 PISTOL   I'll see her damned first, to Pluto's damned lake,
151 by this hand, to the infernal deep, with Erebus and tor-
152 tures vile also. Hold hook and line, say I. Down, down,
153 dogs! Down, faitors! Have we not Hiren here?

154 HOSTESS   Good Captain Peesel, be quiet; 'tis very late, i'
155 faith. I beseek you now, aggravate your choler.

---

136 *truncheon you out* beat you with a club   140 *stewed prunes* (associated
with brothels – "stews" – and considered a cure for venereal disease)   142
occupy fornicate   143–44 *ill sorted* abused, corrupted   148 *tear her* rip her
apart   150 *Pluto's damned lake* the river of the god of the underworld   151
Erebus the underworld   152 *Hold . . . line* (a fishing proverb, meaning "may
all go well")   153 *faitors* impostors; *Have . . . here?* (a line from a lost play by
Peele, and a reference to his sword ["iron"]; Pistol garbles references to contemporary dramas throughout)   154 *Peesel* (a pronunciation of Pistol that
associates it with pizzle and piss)   155 *beseek* i.e., beseech; *aggravate* i.e.,
moderate

PISTOL
These be good humors, indeed! Shall packhorses
And hollow pampered jades of Asia,   157
Which cannot go but thirty mile a day,
Compare with Caesars, and with Cannibals,
And Trojan Greeks? Nay, rather damn them with   160
King Cerberus, and let the welkin roar.   161
Shall we fall foul for toys?   162

HOSTESS By my troth, captain, these are very bitter
words.

BARDOLPH Be gone, good ancient. This will grow to a
brawl anon.

PISTOL Die men like dogs! Give crowns like pins! Have   167
we not Hiren here?

HOSTESS O' my word, captain, there's none such here.   169
What the good-year! Do you think I would deny her?   170
For God's sake, be quiet.

PISTOL
Then feed, and be fat, my fair Calipolis.   172
Come, give's some sack.
"Si fortune me tormente, sperato me contento."   174
Fear we broadsides? No, let the fiend give fire.   175
Give me some sack. And, sweetheart, lie thou there.
  [Lays down his sword.]
Come we to full points here, and are etceteras nothing?   177

157–158 *And . . . day* (a misquotation from Marlow's *Tamburlaine, Part Two* [4.3.1–7])   160 *Trojan Greeks* (Pistol conflates Trojans and Greeks in his exorbitant catalogue of formidable warriors)   161 *Cereberus* the three-headed guard dog of the gates of Hades; *welkin* heavens   162 *Shall . . . toys?* Shall we quarrel over trifles?   167 *Give . . . pins* i.e., give out crowns (the reward for battle) as if they were legion (Pistol shrugs off danger)   169 *O' . . . here* (the Hostess mistakes Hiren [iron] for a denizen of the tavern)   170 *deny her* deny that she was here   172 *Then . . . Calipolis* (a garbled version of another Peele play, *The Battle of Alcazar)*   174 *Si . . . contento* (a muddled Spanish and Italian rendition of a proverb meaning "If fortune torments me, hope contents me")   175 *broadsides* cannon or shot fired from the side of a ship   177 *points* stops (is the party to stop?)

FALSTAFF   Pistol, I would be quiet.

179 PISTOL   Sweet knight, I kiss thy neif. What! We have seen
180 the seven stars.

DOLL   For God's sake, thrust him down stairs. I cannot
182 endure such a fustian rascal.

183 PISTOL   Thrust him down stairs! Know we not Galloway
nags?

185 FALSTAFF   Quoit him down, Bardolph, like a shove-groat
shilling. Nay, an a do nothing but speak nothing, a
shall be nothing here.

BARDOLPH   Come, get you down stairs.

PISTOL
189 What! shall we have incision? Shall we imbrue?
[Snatches up his sword.]
190 Then death rock me asleep, abridge my doleful days!
Why, then, let grievous, ghastly, gaping wounds
192 Untwine the Sisters Three! Come, Atropos, I say!

193 HOSTESS   Here's a goodly stuff toward!

FALSTAFF   Give me my rapier, boy.

DOLL   I pray thee, Jack, I pray thee, do not draw.

FALSTAFF   Get you down stairs.
[Draws, and drives Pistol out.]

HOSTESS   Here's a goodly tumult! I'll forswear keeping
198 house afore I'll be in these tirrits and frights. So, murder, I warrant now. Alas, alas! Put up your naked
200 weapons, put up your naked weapons.
[Exeunt Pistol and Bardolph.]

DOLL   I pray thee, Jack, be quiet; the rascal's gone. Ah,
you whoreson little valiant villain, you!

HOSTESS   Are you not hurt i' the groin? Methought a
made a shrewd thrust at your belly.

---

179 *neif* fist   180 *seven stars* Pleiades (Pistol implies that he and Falstaff
have often reveled into the wee hours)   182 *fustian* worthless   183 *Galloway* Irish (i.e., second-rate)   185 *Quoit* throw (from the game "quoits")
189 *imbrue* shed blood   192 *Sisters Three* the Fates (of whom Atropos, who
severed the thread of life, was one)   193 *toward* coming   198 *tirrits* temper
tantrums

[Enter Bardolph.]

FALSTAFF Have you turned him out o' doors?

BARDOLPH Yea, sir. The rascal's drunk. You have hurt him, sir, i' the shoulder.

FALSTAFF A rascal! to brave me!   208

DOLL Ah, you sweet little rogue, you! Alas, poor ape, how thou sweatest! Come, let me wipe thy face; come *210* on, you whoreson chops. Ah, rogue! i' faith, I love thee. *211* Thou art as valorous as Hector of Troy, worth five of *212* Agamemnon, and ten times better than the Nine Wor- *213* thies. Ah, villain!

FALSTAFF A rascally slave! I will toss the rogue in a *215* blanket.

DOLL Do, an thou darest for thy heart. An thou dost, I'll canvass thee between a pair of sheets.   218

Enter Music.

PAGE The music is come, sir.

FALSTAFF Let them play. Play, sirs. Sit on my knee, Doll. *220* A rascal bragging slave! The rogue fled from me like quicksilver.

DOLL I' faith, and thou followedst him like a church. *223* Thou whoreson little tidy Bartholomew boar-pig, *224* when wilt thou leave fighting o' days and foining o' *225* nights, and begin to patch up thine old body for heaven?

Enter [behind] Prince [Henry] and Poins [disguised].

FALSTAFF Peace, good Doll! Do not speak like a death's- *228* head. Do not bid me remember mine end.

---

208 *brave* challenge **211** *whoreson chops* plump-cheeked rascal **212** *Hector of Troy* (valiant leader of the Trojans) **213** *Agamemnon* (Greek leader in the Trojan war) **213–14** *Nine Worthies* (the nine renowned heroic figures: Hector, Alexander, Julius Caesar, Joshua, David, Judas Maccabeus, Arthur, Charlemagne, and Godfrey of Bouillon) **215–16** *toss . . . blanket* (a punishment for cowards and thieves) **218** *canvass* toss (with sexual suggestion) **223** *thou . . . church* a puzzling phrase; either (1) you didn't move, or (2) you were not very nimble **224** *Bartholomew boar-pig* (a delicacy at Bartholomew fair, annually August 24) **225** *foining* stabbing, thrusting **228–29** *death's-head* (a skull often served as a memento mori, a reminder of death)

230 DOLL   Sirrah, what humor's the prince of?

FALSTAFF   A good shallow young fellow. A would have
232   made a good pantler, a would ha' chipped bread well.

DOLL   They say Poins has a good wit.

FALSTAFF   He a good wit? Hang him, baboon! His wit's
235   as thick as Tewkesbury mustard. There's no more
236   conceit in him than is in a mallet.

DOLL   Why does the prince love him so, then?

FALSTAFF   Because their legs are both of a bigness, and a
239   plays at quoits well, and eats conger and fennel, and
240   drinks off candles' ends for flap-dragons, and rides the
241   wild-mare with the boys, and jumps upon joined-stools,
   and swears with a good grace, and wears his boots very
243   smooth, like unto the sign of the leg, and breeds no bate
244   with telling of discreet stories; and such other gambol
   faculties a has, that show a weak mind and an able
   body, for the which the prince admits him. For the
   prince himself is such another; the weight of a hair will
248   turn the scales between their avoirdupois.

249 PRINCE   Would not this nave of a wheel have his ears cut
250   off?

POINS   Let's beat him before his whore.

252 PRINCE   Look, whether the withered elder hath not his
253   poll clawed like a parrot.

POINS   Is it not strange that desire should so many years
   outlive performance?

---

230 *humor* temperament, personality   232 *pantler* pantryman; *chipped
bread* cut off the crusts   235 *Tewkesbury mustard* (renowned for its sharp fla-
vor – unlike Poins's wit)   236 *conceit* wit; *mallet* heavy wooden hammer
239 *quoits* a game in which metal rings are thrown at a pin in the ground;
conger and fennel an eel thought to blunt the wit seasoned with the aromatic
herb   240 *drinks... dragons* (flap-dragon was a drinking game that involved drinking liquid that had burning floating objects – such as lit candles – in it)   241 *wild-mare* (1) seesaw, (2) a game where boys jump on the
backs of others until the latter collapse   243 *like... leg* tight-fitting like a
bootmaker's sign; *bate* quarrel   244 *gambol* playful   248 *avoirdupois* weight
249 *nave* hub (with a play on "knave," scoundrel)   252 *withered elder* (1)
old man, (2) blasted tree   253 *poll... parrot* (Doll is rumpling his hair)

FALSTAFF   Kiss me, Doll.

PRINCE   Saturn and Venus this year in conjunction! 257
What says the almanac to that?

POINS   And look whether the fiery Trigon, his man, be 259
not lisping to his master's old tables, his notebook, his 260
counsel-keeper.

FALSTAFF   Thou dost give me flattering busses. 262

DOLL   By my troth, I kiss thee with a most constant
heart.

FALSTAFF   I am old, I am old.

DOLL   I love thee better than I love e'er a scurvy young
boy of them all.

FALSTAFF   What stuff wilt have a kirtle of? I shall receive 268
money o' Thursday. Shalt have a cap tomorrow. A
merry song, come. It grows late; we'll to bed. Thou'lt 270
forget me when I am gone.

DOLL   By my troth, thou'lt set me a-weeping, an thou
sayest so. Prove that ever I dress myself handsome till
thy return. Well, hearken a' th' end. 274

FALSTAFF   Some sack, Francis.

PRINCE, POINS   Anon, anon, sir. 276
[Come forward.]

FALSTAFF   Ha! a bastard son of the king's? And art not
thou Poins his brother?

PRINCE   Why, thou globe of sinful continents, what a life 279
dost thou lead! 280

FALSTAFF   A better than thou. I am a gentleman, thou art
a drawer. 282

---

257 *Saturn* (the planet that governs old age, as opposed to "Venus," which
governs love and youth)   259 *fiery Trigon* (an allusion to Bardolph's red face;
the signs of the zodiac were divided into four trigons – of earth, air, fire, and
water; Aries, Leo, and Sagittarius were the fiery signs)   260–61 *lisping . . .
keeper* whispering words of love to Falstaff's old confidante   260 *tables* an
appointment diary   262 *busses* kisses   268 *kirtle* skirt   274 *hearken a' th'
end* wait to see the outcome, and then judge   276 *Anon* coming   279 *continents* (1) continents of the earth, (2) contents, (3) container of sin   282
drawer waiter

PRINCE   Very true, sir, and I come to draw you out by the
ears.

HOSTESS   O, the Lord preserve thy good grace! By my
troth, welcome to London. Now, the Lord bless that
sweet face of thine! O Jesu, are you come from Wales?

288 FALSTAFF   Thou whoreson mad compound of majesty,
289   by this light flesh and corrupt blood, thou art welcome.

290 DOLL   How, you fat fool! I scorn you.

POINS   My lord, he will drive you out of your revenge
292   and turn all to a merriment, if you take not the heat.

293 PRINCE   You whoreson candle-mine you, how vilely did
you speak of me even now before this honest, virtuous,
civil gentlewoman!

HOSTESS   God's blessing of your good heart! And so she
is, by my troth.

FALSTAFF   Didst thou hear me?

299 PRINCE   Yea, and you knew me, as you did when you ran
300   away by Gad's Hill. You knew I was at your back, and
spoke it on purpose to try my patience.

FALSTAFF   No, no, no; not so. I did not think thou wast
within hearing.

PRINCE   I shall drive you then to confess the willful
abuse, and then I know how to handle you.

FALSTAFF   No abuse, Hal, o' mine honor, no abuse.

PRINCE   Not to dispraise me and call me pantler and
bread-chipper and I know not what?

FALSTAFF   No abuse, Hal.

310 POINS   No abuse?

FALSTAFF   No abuse, Ned, i' the world. Honest Ned,
none. I dispraised him before the wicked, that the
wicked might not fall in love with him. In which doing,
I have done the part of a careful friend and a true sub-

---

288 *compound* lump   **289** *light . . . blood* i.e., Doll   **292** *if . . . heat* i.e., if
you don't act quickly (while the iron is hot)   **293** *candle-mine* storehouse of
tallow, candle of grease   **299–300** *Yea . . . Hill* (see *1 Henry IV,* II.2, II.4)

ject, and thy father is to give me thanks for it. No abuse,
Hal. None, Ned, none. No, faith, boys, none.

PRINCE See now, whether pure fear and entire cowardice   317
doth not make thee wrong this virtuous gentlewoman
to close with us. Is she of the wicked? Is thine hostess   319
here of the wicked? Or is thy boy of the wicked? Or   320
honest Bardolph, whose zeal burns in his nose, of the
wicked?

POINS Answer, thou dead elm, answer.

FALSTAFF The fiend hath pricked down Bardolph irrecov-   324
erable, and his face is Lucifer's privy-kitchen, where he   325
doth nothing but roast malt-worms. For the boy, there   326
is a good angel about him, but the devil blinds him too.

PRINCE For the women?

FALSTAFF For one of them, she is in hell already, and
burns poor souls. For the other, I owe her money, and   330
whether she be damned for that, I know not.

HOSTESS No, I warrant you.

FALSTAFF No, I think thou are not. I think thou art quit   333
for that. Marry, there is another indictment upon thee,
for suffering flesh to be eaten in thy house, contrary to   335
the law, for the which I think thou wilt howl.   336

HOSTESS All victuallers do so. What's a joint of mutton   337
or two in a whole Lent?

PRINCE You, gentlewoman –

DOLL What says your grace?   340

FALSTAFF His grace says that which his flesh rebels   341
against.

      Peto knocks at door.

HOSTESS Who knocks so loud at door? Look to the door
there, Francis.

---

317 *entire* complete and utter 319 *close* agree 324 *pricked down* chosen
325 *privy* private 326 *malt-worms* topers, drunkards 330 *burns* infects
with venereal disease 333 *quit* (1) repaid (2) forgiven 335–36 *suffering . . . law* allowing meat to be served during Lent 336 *howl* i.e., in hell
337 *victuallers* innkeepers 341–42 *that . . . against* i.e., that which he (and
his body) knows not to be true (that Doll Common is a gentlewoman)

[Enter Peto.]

PRINCE
  Peto, how now? What news?

PETO
  The king your father is at Westminster,
347   And there are twenty weak and wearied posts
  Come from the north. And as I came along
  I met and overtook a dozen captains,
350   Bareheaded, sweating, knocking at the taverns,
  And asking every one for Sir John Falstaff.

PRINCE
  By heaven, Poins, I feel me much to blame,
  So idly to profane the precious time,
354   When tempest of commotion, like the south
355   Borne with black vapor, doth begin to melt
  And drop upon our bare unarmèd heads.
  Give me my sword and cloak. Falstaff, good night.
    Exeunt Prince Henry, Poins [, Peto, and Bardolph].

FALSTAFF   Now comes in the sweetest morsel of the
  night, and we must hence and leave it unpicked.
360   *[Knocking within.]* More knocking at the door!
    [Enter Bardolph.]
  How now! What's the matter?

BARDOLPH
362   You must away to court, sir, presently.
363   A dozen captains stay at door for you.

FALSTAFF   *[To the Page]* Pay the musicians, sirrah. Farewell, hostess. Farewell, Doll. You see, my good wenches,
  how men of merit are sought after. The undeserver
  may sleep when the man of action is called on. Fare-
368   well, good wenches. If I be not sent away post, I will see
  you again ere I go.

370   DOLL   I cannot speak. If my heart be not ready to burst –
  well, sweet Jack, have a care of thyself.

---

347 *posts* messengers 354 *south* south wind 355 *Borne* laden 362
presently instantly 363 *stay* await 368 *post* posthaste, quickly

FALSTAFF   Farewell, farewell.
                                    [Exeunt Falstaff and Bardolph.]
HOSTESS   Well, fare thee well. I have known thee these
twenty-nine years, come peasecod-time, but an hon-   374
ester and truer-hearted man – well, fare thee well.
BARDOLPH   *[Within]* Mistress Tearsheet!
HOSTESS   What's the matter?
BARDOLPH   *[Within]* Bid Mistress Tearsheet come to my
master.
HOSTESS   O, run, Doll, run. Run, good Doll. Come. *[To   380
Bardolph within]* She comes blubbered. Yea, will you   381
come, Doll?   *Exeunt.*

* * *

∾ **III.1**   *Enter the King in his nightgown, alone [with a
Page].*

KING
    Go call the Earls of Surrey and of Warwick.
    But, ere they come, bid them o'erread these letters
    And well consider of them. Make good speed.
                                        [Exit Page.]
    How many thousand of my poorest subjects
    Are at this hour asleep! O sleep, O gentle sleep,
    Nature's soft nurse, how have I frighted thee,
    That thou no more wilt weigh my eyelids down
    And steep my senses in forgetfulness?
    Why rather, sleep, liest thou in smoky cribs,   9
    Upon uneasy pallets stretching thee   10
    And hushed with buzzing night-flies to thy slumber,
    Than in the perfumed chambers of the great,   12
    Under the canopies of costly state,   13

---

374 *peasecod-time* early summer, when sweetpeas bloom and are in pod
381 *blubbered* weeping
    III.1 King Henry's palace   9 *cribs* hovels   10 *uneasy pallets* uncomfort-
able beds; *thee* thyself   12 *great* noble persons   13 *state* magnificence

And lulled with sound of sweetest melody?
15   O thou dull god, why liest thou with the vile
In loathsome beds, and leavest the kingly couch
17   A watch-case or a common 'larum-bell?
Wilt thou upon the high and giddy mast
Seal up the ship-boy's eyes, and rock his brains
20   In cradle of the rude imperious surge
And in the visitation of the winds,
22   Who take the ruffian billows by the top,
Curling their monstrous heads and hanging them
With deafening clamor in the slippery clouds,
25   That, with the hurly, death itself awakes?
Canst thou, O partial sleep, give thy repose
To the wet sea son in an hour so rude,
And in the calmest and most stillest night,
29   With all appliances and means to boot,
30   Deny it to a king? Then happy low, lie down!
Uneasy lies the head that wears a crown.
      Enter Warwick, Surrey, and Sir John Blunt.
WARWICK
Many good morrows to your majesty!
KING
Is it good morrow, lords?
WARWICK
'Tis one o'clock, and past.
KING
Why, then, good morrow to you all, my lords.
Have you read o'er the letters that I sent you?
WARWICK
We have, my liege.
KING
Then you perceive the body of our kingdom

---

15 *dull god* Morpheus, the god of sleep; *vile* lowly   17 *watch-case* sentry box;
'larum-bell alarm bell   22 *Who* which – i.e., the winds   25 *That* so that;
hurly hurly-burly, tumult   29 *appliances* devices, appointments; *to boot* in addition   30 *low* lowly persons

How foul it is, what rank diseases grow,   39
And with what danger, near the heart of it.   40
WARWICK
It is but as a body yet distempered,   41
Which to his former strength may be restored   42
With good advice and little medicine.
My Lord Northumberland will soon be cooled.   44
KING
O God! that one might read the book of fate,
And see the revolution of the times
Make mountains level, and the continent,   47
Weary of solid firmness, melt itself
Into the sea! And other times to see
The beachy girdle of the ocean   50
Too wide for Neptune's hips, how chances mock,   51
And changes fill the cup of alteration
With divers liquors! O, if this were seen,   53
The happiest youth, viewing his progress through,
What perils past, what crosses to ensue,
Would shut the book, and sit him down and die.
'Tis not ten years gone
Since Richard and Northumberland, great friends,
Did feast together, and in two years after
Were they at wars. It is but eight years since   60
This Percy was the man nearest my soul,   61
Who like a brother toiled in my affairs
And laid his love and life under my foot,   63
Yea, for my sake, even to the eyes of Richard
Gave him defiance. But which of you was by –
    [To Warwick]
You, cousin Nevil, as I may remember –   66
When Richard, with his eye brimful of tears,

---

39 *rank* festering   **41** *yet* just; *distempered* ill   **42** *his* its   **44** *cooled* cooled
off, subdued   **47** *continent* dry land   **51** *Too wide* i.e., when the ocean re-
cedes   **53** *divers* different   **61** *Percy* i.e., Northumberland   **63** *under my*
foot at my disposal   **66** *Nevil* (the family name of the Earl of Warwick at this
juncture was in fact Beauchamps)

68 Then checked and rated by Northumberland,
Did speak these words, now proved a prophecy?
70 "Northumberland, thou ladder by the which
My cousin Bolingbroke ascends my throne" –
Though then, God knows, I had no such intent,
But that necessity so bowed the state
That I and greatness were compelled to kiss –
75 "The time shall come," thus did he follow it,
76 "The time will come that foul sin, gathering head,
Shall break into corruption." So went on,
Foretelling this same time's condition
And the division of our amity.

WARWICK
80 There is a history in all men's lives,
81 Figuring the nature of the times deceased,
The which observed, a man may prophesy,
83 With a near aim, of the main chance of things
As yet not come to life, which in their seeds
And weak beginnings lie intreasurèd.
86 Such things become the hatch and brood of time,
And by the necessary form of this
King Richard might create a perfect guess
That great Northumberland, then false to him,
90 Would of that seed grow to a greater falseness,
Which should not find a ground to root upon,
Unless on you.

KING   Are these things then necessities?
Then let us meet them like necessities.
94 And that same word even now cries out on us.
They say the bishop and Northumberland
Are fifty thousand strong.

---

68 *rated* berated   75 *follow it* continue   76 *gathering head* coming to a head
81 *Figuring* revealing   83 *main chance* general probability   86 *hatch and brood* spawn, offspring   94 *cries out* denounces us

WARWICK   It cannot be, my lord.
　Rumor doth double, like the voice and echo,
　The numbers of the feared. Please it your grace
　To go to bed. Upon my soul, my lord,
　The powers that you already have sent forth   *100*
　Shall bring this prize in very easily.
　To comfort you the more, I have received
　A certain instance that Glendower is dead.   *103*
　Your majesty hath been this fortnight ill,
　And these unseasoned hours perforce must add   *105*
　Unto your sickness.
KING   I will take your counsel.
　And were these inward wars once out of hand,   *107*
　We would, dear lords, unto the Holy Land.

                                        Exeunt.

                       *

∾ **III.2** *Enter Justice Shallow and Justice Silence [with*
　　Mouldy, Shadow, Wart, Feeble, Bullcalf].

SHALLOW Come on, come on, come on, sir. Give me
　your hand, sir, give me your hand, sir; an early stirrer,
　by the rood! And how doth my good cousin Silence?   *3*
SILENCE Good morrow, good cousin Shallow.
SHALLOW And how doth my cousin, your bedfellow?
　And your fairest daughter and mine, my god-daughter
　Ellen?
SILENCE Alas, a black ousel, cousin Shallow!   *8*
SHALLOW By yea and no, sir, I dare say my cousin   *9*
　William is become a good scholar. He is at Oxford still, *10*
　is he not?

───────

103 *instance* proof 105 *unseasoned* late, odd 107 *inward* civil; *out of
hand* over with
　　III.2 Before Shallow's house in Gloucestershire 3 *rood* cross 8 *ousel*
blackbird (thus not fair) 9 *cousin* kinsman

SILENCE   Indeed, sir, to my cost.

13 SHALLOW   A must, then, to the Inns o' Court shortly. I
14 was once of Clement's Inn, where I think they will talk
of mad Shallow yet.

SILENCE   You were called "lusty Shallow" then, cousin.

SHALLOW   By the mass, I was called anything. And I
18 would have done anything indeed too, and roundly too.
There was I, and little John Doit of Staffordshire, and
20 black George Barnes, and Francis Pickbone, and Will
21 Squele, a Cotswold man; you had not four such swinge-
bucklers in all the Inns o' Court again. And I may
23 say to you we knew where the bona-robas were and
24 had the best of them all at commandment. Then was
Jack Falstaff, now Sir John, a boy, and page to Thomas
Mowbray, Duke of Norfolk.

SILENCE   This Sir John, cousin, that comes hither anon
about soldiers?

SHALLOW   The same Sir John, the very same. I see him
30 break Skogan's head at the court-gate, when a was a
31 crack not thus high. And the very same day did I fight
32 with one Sampson Stockfish, a fruiterer, behind Gray's
Inn. Jesu, Jesu, the mad days that I have spent! And to
see how many of my old acquaintance are dead!

SILENCE   We shall all follow, cousin.

SHALLOW   Certain, 'tis certain, very sure, very sure.
37 Death, as the Psalmist saith, is certain to all, all shall die.
38 How a good yoke of bullocks at Stamford fair?

SILENCE   By my troth, I was not there.

40 SHALLOW   Death is certain. Is old Double of your town
living yet?

---

13 *Inns o' Court* law schools   14 *Clement's Inn* (one of the Inns of Chancery,
which were in Shallow's time preparatory to the Inns of Court)   18 *roundly*
with a vengeance   20 *black* dark-haired   21–22 *swinge-bucklers* swashbuck-
lers   23 *bona-robas* girls   24 *at commandment* at will   31 *crack* whipper-
snapper   32 *fruiterer* fruit seller   37 *Death . . . die* see Psalms 89:48   38
How how much is

SILENCE Dead, sir.

SHALLOW   Jesu, Jesu, dead! A drew a good bow, and
dead! A shot a fine shoot. John a Gaunt loved him well   44
and betted much money on his head. Dead! A would
have clapped i' the clout at twelve score, and carried   46
you a forehand shaft a fourteen and fourteen and a half,
that it would have done a man's heart good to see. How
a score of ewes now?

SILENCE   Thereafter as they be. A score of good ewes may   50
be worth ten pounds.

SHALLOW   And is old Double dead?

SILENCE   Here come two of Sir John Falstaff's men, as I
think.

 Enter Bardolph and one with him.

[SHALLOW]   Good morrow, honest gentlemen.

BARDOLPH   I beseech you, which is Justice Shallow?

SHALLOW   I am Robert Shallow, sir, a poor esquire of this   57
county, and one of the king's justices of the peace.
What is your good pleasure with me?

BARDOLPH   My captain, sir, commends him to you, my   60
captain, Sir John Falstaff, a tall gentleman, by heaven,   61
and a most gallant leader.

SHALLOW   He greets me well, sir. I knew him a good
backsword man. How doth the good knight? May I ask   64
how my lady his wife doth?

BARDOLPH   Sir, pardon, a soldier is better accommodated than with a wife.

SHALLOW   It is well said, in faith, sir, and it is well said
indeed too. Better accommodated! It is good, yea, in-   69
deed, is it. Good phrases are surely, and ever were, very   70

---

44 *shoot* (of arrows); *John a Gaunt* father of Henry IV   46 *clapped . . . score*
hit the mark at 240 yards   46–47 *carried . . . half* could shoot a heavy arrow
point blank (rather than in an arc) so that it carried 280 or 290 yards   50
Thereafter . . . be it depends on their quality   57 *esquire* (social rank just
below that of knight)   61 *tall* valiant   64 *backsword* stick with a basket hilt
used in place of a sword in fencing   69 *accommodated* provided

commendable. Accommodated! It comes of "accommodo." Very good, a good phrase.

BARDOLPH Pardon me, sir. I have heard the word. Phrase call you it? By this good day, I know not the phrase, but I will maintain the word with my sword to
76   be a soldierlike word, and a word of exceeding good command, by heaven. Accommodated, that is, when a man is, as they say, accommodated; or when a man is, being, whereby a may be thought to be accommodated,
80   which is an excellent thing.

Enter Sir John Falstaff.

81 SHALLOW It is very just. Look, here comes good Sir John. Give me your good hand, give me your worship's
83   good hand. By my troth, you like well and bear your years very well. Welcome, good Sir John.

FALSTAFF I am glad to see you well, good Master Robert Shallow. Master Surecard, as I think?

87 SHALLOW No, Sir John, it is my cousin Silence, in commission with me.

FALSTAFF Good Master Silence, it well befits you should
90   be of the peace.

SILENCE Your good worship is welcome.

FALSTAFF Fie! This is hot weather, gentlemen. Have you
93   provided me here half a dozen sufficient men?

SHALLOW Marry, have we, sir. Will you sit?

FALSTAFF Let me see them, I beseech you.

SHALLOW Where's the roll? Where's the roll? Where's the roll? Let me see, let me see, let me see. So, so, so, so, so, so, so. Yea, marry, sir. Ralph Mouldy! Let them appear as I call, let them do so, let them do so. Let me see,
100   where is Mouldy?

MOULDY Here, an't please you.

76–77 *exceeding good command* fine military term 81 *just* true 83 *like* thrive 87–88 *in . . . me* like me a holder of a commission as justice of the peace 93 *sufficient* able

SHALLOW What think you, Sir John? A good-limbed
fellow, young, strong, and of good friends.   103

FALSTAFF Is thy name Mouldy?

MOULDY Yea, an't please you.

FALSTAFF 'Tis the more time thou wert used.

SHALLOW Ha, ha, ha! most excellent, i' faith! Things
that are moldy lack use. Very singular good! In faith,
well said, Sir John, very well said.

[FALSTAFF Prick him.]   110

MOULDY I was pricked well enough before, an you could
have let me alone. My old dame will be undone now   112
for one to do her husbandry and her drudgery. You   113
need not to have pricked me. There are other men fitter
to go out than I.

FALSTAFF Go to. Peace, Mouldy, you shall go. Mouldy, it
is time you were spent.   117

MOULDY Spent!

SHALLOW Peace, fellow, peace. Stand aside. Know you
where you are? For the other, Sir John, let me see.   120
Simon Shadow!

FALSTAFF Yea, marry, let me have him to sit under. He's
like to be a cold soldier.   123

SHALLOW Where's Shadow?

SHADOW Here, sir.

FALSTAFF Shadow, whose son art thou?

SHADOW My mother's son, sir.   127

FALSTAFF Thy mother's son! Like enough, and thy
father's shadow. So the son of the female is the shadow   129
of the male. It is often so, indeed, but much of the   130
father's substance!

SHALLOW Do you like him, Sir John?

---

103 *friends* family, stock   110 *Prick* choose (with suggestion of sexual intercourse)   112 *dame* mother or wife; *undone* at a loss   113 *husbandry* farm-
ing   117 *spent* (1) used up, (2) ejaculated, sexually exhausted   123 *cold* (1)
determined, (2) cowardly   127 *son* (with play on "sun")   129 *shadow* (Falstaff implies he is a poor copy of his father – i.e., that his mother was unfaithful)

133 FALSTAFF   Shadow will serve for summer. Prick him, for
134   we have a number of shadows to fill up the muster-
         book.
       SHALLOW   Thomas Wart!
       FALSTAFF   Where's he?
       WART   Here, sir.
       FALSTAFF   Is thy name Wart?
140 WART   Yea, sir.
       FALSTAFF   Thou art a very ragged wart.
       SHALLOW   Shall I prick him down, Sir John?
       FALSTAFF   It were superfluous, for his apparel is built
144   upon his back and the whole frame stands upon pins.
         Prick him no more.
146 SHALLOW   Ha, ha, ha! you can do it, sir, you can do it. I
         commend you well. Francis Feeble!
       FEEBLE   Here, sir.
       SHALLOW   What trade art thou, Feeble?
150 FEEBLE   A woman's tailor, sir.
       SHALLOW   Shall I prick him, sir?
152 FALSTAFF   You may. But if he had been a man's tailor,
153   he'd a' pricked you. Wilt thou make as many holes in
154   an enemy's battle as thou hast done in a woman's petti-
         coat?
       FEEBLE   I will do my good will, sir. You can have no
         more.
       FALSTAFF   Well said, good woman's tailor! Well said,
         courageous Feeble! Thou wilt be as valiant as the wrath-
160   ful dove or most magnanimous mouse. Prick the
         woman's tailor well, Master Shallow, deep, Master Shal-
         low.
       FEEBLE   I would Wart might have gone, sir.

───────

133 *serve* suffice, do   134 *shadows* names of nonexistent men for whom the
commanding officer received pay   144 *stands* depends   146 *you . . . it* you
know how to do it   152 *tailor* (considered effeminate)   153 *pricked* (1)
dressed, (2) penetrated   154 *battle* army   160 *magnanimous* stouthearted

FALSTAFF   I would thou wert a man's tailor, that thou
  mightst mend him and make him fit to go. I cannot
  put him to a private soldier that is the leader of so
  many thousands. Let that suffice, most forcible Feeble.   167
FEEBLE   It shall suffice, sir.
FALSTAFF   I am bound to thee, reverend Feeble. Who is
  next?   170
SHALLOW   Peter Bullcalf o' the green!
FALSTAFF   Yea, marry, let's see Bullcalf.
BULLCALF   Here, sir.
FALSTAFF   'Fore God, a likely fellow! Come, prick Bull-
  calf till he roar again.   175
BULLCALF   O Lord! good my lord captain –
FALSTAFF   What, dost thou roar before thou art pricked?
BULLCALF   O Lord, sir! I am a diseased man.
FALSTAFF   What disease hast thou?
BULLCALF   A whoreson cold, sir, a cough, sir, which I   180
  caught with ringing in the king's affairs upon his coro-   181
  nation day, sir.
FALSTAFF   Come, thou shalt go to the wars in a gown.   183
  We will have away thy cold, and I will take such order   184
  that thy friends shall ring for thee. Is here all?   185
SHALLOW   Here is two more called than your number.
  You must have but four here, sir. And so, I pray you, go
  in with me to dinner.
FALSTAFF   Come, I will go drink with you, but I cannot
  tarry dinner. I am glad to see you, by my troth, Master   190
  Shallow.
SHALLOW   O, Sir John, do you remember since we lay all   192
  night in the Windmill in Saint George's Field?   193

---

167 *thousands* i.e., of lice   175 *roar* bellow like a bull   181–82 *ringing . . .
day* ringing church bells in celebration of the anniversary of the king's coronation   183 *gown* bathrobe   184 *have* do; *take such order* arrange   185
ring for thee i.e., at his death   190 *tarry* wait for   192 *since* when   193
Windmill a brothel

FALSTAFF   No more of that, good Master Shallow, no
more of that.

SHALLOW   Ha! 'Twas a merry night. And is Jane Nightwork alive?

FALSTAFF   She lives, Master Shallow.

199   SHALLOW   She never could away with me.

200   FALSTAFF   Never, never, she would always say she could
not abide Master Shallow.

SHALLOW   By the mass, I could anger her to the heart.
She was then a bona-roba. Doth she hold her own well?

FALSTAFF   Old, old, Master Shallow.

SHALLOW   Nay, she must be old. She cannot choose but
be old. Certain she's old, and had Robin Nightwork by
old Nightwork before I came to Clement's Inn.

SILENCE   That's fifty-five year ago.

SHALLOW   Ha, cousin Silence, that thou hadst seen that
210   that this knight and I have seen! Ha, Sir John, said I
well?

FALSTAFF   We have heard the chimes at midnight, Master
Shallow.

SHALLOW   That we have, that we have, that we have, in
215   faith, Sir John, we have. Our watchword was "Hem,
boys!" Come, let's to dinner, come, let's to dinner.
Jesus, the days that we have seen! Come, come.

Exeunt [Falstaff and the Justices].

218   BULLCALF   Good Master Corporate Bardolph, stand my
219   friend, and here's four Harry ten-shillings in French
220   crowns for you. In very truth, sir, I had as lief be
hanged, sir, as go. And yet for mine own part, sir, I do
not care, but rather, because I am unwilling, and, for
mine own part, have a desire to stay with my friends.
Else, sir, I did not care, for mine own part, so much.

---

199 *away with* tolerate   **215–16** *Hem, boys!* drink up   **218** *Corporate* i.e.,
corporal; *stand* be   **219–20** *four . . . crowns* (an anachronism; the Harry
ten-shilling piece was coined in the reign of Henry VII – i.e., 1485–1508)
220 *lief* rather

BARDOLPH   Go to, stand aside.

MOULDY   And, good master corporal captain, for my old
dame's sake, stand my friend. She has nobody to do
anything about her when I am gone, and she is old, and
cannot help herself. You shall have forty, sir.   229

BARDOLPH   Go to, stand aside.   230

FEEBLE   By my troth, I care not. A man can die but once.
We owe God a death. I'll ne'er bear a base mind. An't   232
be my destiny, so. An't be not, so. No man is too good
to serve's prince. And let it go which way it will, he that   234
dies this year is quit for the next.   235

BARDOLPH   Well said. Thou'rt a good fellow.

FEEBLE   Faith, I'll bear no base mind.

Enter Falstaff and the Justices.

FALSTAFF   Come, sir, which men shall I have?

SHALLOW   Four of which you please.

BARDOLPH   Sir, a word with you. I have three pound to   240
free Mouldy and Bullcalf.

FALSTAFF   Go to, well.

SHALLOW   Come, Sir John, which four will you have?

FALSTAFF   Do you choose for me.

SHALLOW   Marry, then, Mouldy, Bullcalf, Feeble, and
Shadow.

FALSTAFF   Mouldy and Bullcalf. For you, Mouldy, stay at
home till you are past service. And for your part, Bullcalf, grow till you come unto it. I will none of you.

SHALLOW   Sir John, Sir John, do not yourself wrong.   250
They are your likeliest men, and I would have you
served with the best.

FALSTAFF   Will you tell me, Master Shallow, how to
choose a man? Care I for the limb, the thews, the   254
stature, bulk, and big assemblance of a man! Give me   255
the spirit, Master Shadow. Here's Wart. You see what a

---

229 *forty* probably forty shillings, two pounds   **232** *base* low   **234** *serve's*
serve his   **235** *quit* free   **254** *thews* strength   **255** *assemblance* appearance

257 ragged appearance it is. A shall charge you and dis-
258 charge you with the motion of a pewterer's hammer,
259 come off and on swifter than he that gibbets on the
260 brewer's bucket. And this same half-faced fellow,
261 Shadow. Give me this man. He presents no mark to the
262 enemy; the foeman may with as great aim level at the
edge of a penknife. And for a retreat, how swiftly will
this Feeble the woman's tailor run off! O, give me the
spare men, and spare me the great ones. Put me a
266 caliver into Wart's hand, Bardolph.

267 BARDOLPH   Hold, Wart, traverse. Thus, thus, thus.

FALSTAFF   Come, manage me your caliver. So. Very well.
Go to. Very good, exceeding good. O, give me always a
270 little, lean, old, chopped, bald shot. Well said, i' faith,
271 Wart. Thou'rt a good scab. Hold, there's a tester for
thee.

SHALLOW   He is not his craft's master, he doth not do it
right. I remember at Mile-end Green, when I lay at
275 Clement's Inn – I was then Sir Dagonet in Arthur's
276 show – there was a little quiver fellow, and a would
277 manage you his piece thus, and a would about and
about, and come you in and come you in. "Rah, tah,
279 tah," would a say, "Bounce," would a say, and away
280 again would a go, and again would a come. I shall ne'er
see such a fellow.

FALSTAFF   These fellows will do well, Master Shallow.
God keep you, Master Silence. I will not use many
words with you. Fare you well, gentlemen both. I thank

257–58 *charge . . . you* load and fire   258 *motion . . . hammer* i.e., quickly
259–60 *gibbets . . . bucket* hangs the pails of brew on the yoke of the carrier
260 *half-faced* as on a coin, thin   261 *mark* target   262 *level* aim   266
caliver light musket   267 *traverse* (1) march to and fro, (2) hold the weapon
across your body (?)   270 *chopped* chapped, dried up   271 *scab* rascal (with
pun on "wart"); *tester* sixpence   275–75 *Sir . . . show* King Arthur's fool in
an annual archery exhibition in which Arthurian figures were impersonated
276 *quiver* nimble   277 *piece* weapon   279 *Bounce* bang

you. I must a dozen mile tonight. Bardolph, give the
soldiers coats.

SHALLOW   Sir John, the Lord bless you! God prosper
your affairs! God send us peace! At your return visit our
house, let our old acquaintance be renewed. Peradven-
ture I will with ye to the court.   *290*

FALSTAFF   'Fore God, would you would, Master Shallow.

SHALLOW   Go to, I have spoke at a word. God keep you.   *292*

FALSTAFF   Fare you well, gentle gentlemen. *Exeunt [Jus-
tices].* On, Bardolph, lead the men away. *[Exeunt all but
Falstaff.]* As I return, I will fetch off these justices. I do   *295*
see the bottom of Justice Shallow. Lord, Lord, how sub-   *296*
ject we old men are to this vice of lying! This same
starved justice hath done nothing but prate to me of
the wildness of his youth and the feats he hath done
about Turnbull Street, and every third word a lie, duer   *300*
paid to the hearer than the Turk's tribute. I do re-   *301*
member him at Clement's Inn like a man made after
supper of a cheese-paring. When a was naked, he was,
for all the world, like a forked radish, with a head
fantastically carved upon it with a knife. A was so
forlorn that his dimensions to any thick sight   *306*
were invincible. A was the very genius of famine, yet   *307*
lecherous as a monkey, and the whores called him
mandrake. A came ever in the rearward of the fashion,   *309*
and sung those tunes to the overscutched huswives that   *310*
he heard the carmen whistle, and sware they were his   *311*
fancies or his good-nights. And now is this vice's dagger   *312*

---

292 *I . . . word* I mean it   295 *fetch off* take advantage of, fleece   296 *see
the bottom* see through, take the measure   300 *duer* more promptly   301
Turk's tribute money exacted by the Sultan of Turkey from merchants, etc.
306 *thick* weak, dull   307 *invincible* i.e., invisible; *genius* epitome, spirit
309 *mandrake* a plant root thought to resemble a man; *rearward* wake   310
overscutched huswives worn-out hussies   311 *carmen* wagon drivers
311–11 *his fancies* his own musical compositions or serenades   312–12
Vice's dagger wooden dagger carried by vice figure in a morality play

become a squire, and talks as familiarly of John a Gaunt
as if he had been sworn brother to him, and I'll be
315 sworn a ne'er saw him but once in the Tilt-yard, and
316 then he burst his head for crowding among the marshal's men. I saw it, and told John a Gaunt he beat his
own name, for you might have thrust him and all his
319 apparel into an eel-skin, the case of a treble hautboy
320 was a mansion for him, a court. And now has he land
and beefs. Well, I'll be acquainted with him, if I return,
322 and 't shall go hard but I will make him a philosopher's
323 two stones to me. If the young dace be a bait for the old
pike, I see no reason in the law of nature but I may
snap at him. Let time shape, and there an end.   *Exit.*

✳

~ **IV.1** *Enter the Archbishop [of York], Mowbray, Hastings [and others], within the Forest of Gaultree.*

ARCHBISHOP
What is this forest called?
HASTINGS
'Tis Gaultree Forest, an't shall please your grace.
ARCHBISHOP
3   Here stand, my lords, and send discoverers forth
To know the numbers of our enemies.
HASTINGS
We have sent forth already.
ARCHBISHOP   'Tis well done.
My friends and brethren in these great affairs,

---

315 *Tilt-yard* jousting arena   316–16 *burst . . . men* got his head beaten for
shoving   319 *case* i.e., for a musical instrument like the oboe   322–22
't . . . me I'll get money out of him or else (the philosopher's stone was believed to turn base metal to gold, and to preserve health and life)   323 *dace*
small fish used as live bait
    IV.1 Within Gaultree Forest (a royal forest of Yorkshire)   3 *discoverers*
scouts

I must acquaint you that I have received
New-dated letters from Northumberland,
Their cold intent, tenor, and substance, thus:
Here doth he wish his person, with such powers   10
As might hold sortance with his quality,   11
The which he could not levy. Whereupon
He is retired, to ripe his growing fortunes,   13
To Scotland, and concludes in hearty prayers
That your attempts may overlive the hazard   15
And fearful meeting of their opposite.   16

MOWBRAY
Thus do the hopes we have in him touch ground
And dash themselves to pieces.
    Enter a Messenger.

HASTINGS   Now, what news?

MESSENGER
West of this forest, scarcely off a mile,
In goodly form comes on the enemy,   20
And, by the ground they hide, I judge their number   21
Upon or near the rate of thirty thousand.   22

MOWBRAY
The just proportion that we gave them out.   23
Let us sway on and face them in the field.   24

ARCHBISHOP
What well-appointed leader fronts us here?   25
    Enter Westmoreland.

MOWBRAY
I think it is my Lord of Westmoreland.

WESTMORELAND
Health and fair greeting from our general,
The prince, Lord John and Duke of Lancaster.

---

10 *powers* forces   **11** *hold sortance* be suited to; *quality* station, rank   **13** *ripe* ripen, increase   **15** *overlive the hazard* survive the danger   **16** *opposite* enemy   **20** *form* formation   **21** *hide* cover   **22** *rate* estimate   **23** *just . . . out* exact number we estimated   **24** *sway* move   **25** *fronts* faces

ARCHBISHOP
    Say on, my Lord of Westmoreland, in peace.
30   What doth concern your coming?
WESTMORELAND   Then, my lord,
31   Unto your grace do I in chief address
    The substance of my speech. If that rebellion
33   Came like itself, in base and abject routs,
34   Led on by bloody youth, guarded with rags,
35   And countenanced by boys and beggary,
36   I say, if damned commotion so appeared,
    In his true, native and most proper shape,
    You, reverend father, and these noble lords
    Had not been here, to dress the ugly form
40   Of base and bloody insurrection
    With your fair honors. You, lord archbishop,
42   Whose see is by a civil peace maintained,
    Whose beard the silver hand of peace hath touched,
    Whose learning and good letters peace hath tutored,
45   Whose white investments figure innocence,
    The dove and very blessèd spirit of peace,
47   Wherefore do you so ill translate yourself
    Out of the speech of peace that bears such grace,
    Into the harsh and boisterous tongue of war,
50   Turning your books to graves, your ink to blood,
    Your pens to lances, and your tongue divine
52   To a loud trumpet and a point of war?
ARCHBISHOP
    Wherefore do I this? So the question stands.
    Briefly to this end: we are all diseased,
55   [And with our surfeiting and wanton hours
    Have brought ourselves into a burning fever,
57   And we must bleed for it. Of which disease

---

31 *in chief* chiefly   33 *routs* mobs   34 *guarded* trimmed   35 *countenanced* supported; *beggary* beggars   36 *commotion* rebellion   42 *see* diocese   45 *investments* vestments, priest's clothing; *figure* denote, symbolize   47 *translate* transform   52 *point of war* trumpet battle cry   55 *surfeiting* gluttonous, wantonly self-indulgent   57 *bleed* be bled; *disease* i.e., Bolingbroke's power

Our late king, Richard, being infected, died.
But, my most noble Lord of Westmoreland,
I take not on me here as a physician,   60
Nor do I as an enemy to peace
Troop in the throngs of military men,
But rather show awhile like fearful war,   63
To diet rank minds sick of happiness   64
And purge the obstructions which begin to stop
Our very veins of life. Hear me more plainly.
I have in equal balance justly weighed   67
What wrongs our arms may do, what wrongs we suffer,
And find our griefs heavier than our offenses.   69
We see which way the stream of time doth run,   70
And are enforced from our most quiet there   71
By the rough torrent of occasion,   72
And have the summary of all our griefs,
When time shall serve, to show in articles;   74
Which long ere this we offered to the king,
And might by no suit gain our audience.   76
When we are wronged and would unfold our griefs,
We are denied access unto his person
Even by those men that most have done us wrong.]
The dangers of the days but newly gone,   80
Whose memory is written on the earth
With yet appearing blood, and the examples   82
Of every minute's instance, present now,   83
Hath put us in these ill-beseeming arms,
Not to break peace or any branch of it,
But to establish here a peace indeed,
Concurring both in name and quality.   87
WESTMORELAND
  When ever yet was your appeal denied?

---

60 *take . . . as* do not assume the role of **63** *show* appear **64** *rank* obese,
bloated **67** *in equal balance* in fair scales **69** *griefs* injuries, grievances **71**
most quiet peace **72** *occasion* circumstances **74** *articles* lists **76** *suit* making suit, suing **82** *yet* still **83** *Of . . . instance* arising every minute **87**
Concurring . . . quality i.e., whose character suits the name

89   Wherein have you been gallèd by the king?
90   What peer hath been suborned to grate on you,
     That you should seal this lawless bloody book
     Of forged rebellion with a seal divine
     And consecrate commotion's bitter edge?

ARCHBISHOP
94   My brother general, the commonwealth,
95   To brother born an household cruelty,
     I make my quarrel in particular.

WESTMORELAND
     There is no need of any such redress,
     Or if there were, it not belongs to you.

MOWBRAY
     Why not to him in part, and to us all
100   That feel the bruises of the days before,
     And suffer the condition of these times
102   To lay a heavy and unequal hand
     Upon our honors?

WESTMORELAND   [O, my good Lord Mowbray,
104   Construe the times to their necessities,
     And you shall say indeed, it is the time,
     And not the king, that doth you injuries.
     Yet for your part, it not appears to me
     Either from the king or in the present time
     That you should have an inch of any ground
110   To build a grief on. Were you not restored
     To all the Duke of Norfolk's signories,
     Your noble and right well remembered father's?

MOWBRAY
     What thing, in honor, had my father lost,

---

89 *gallèd* made sore, annoyed   90 *suborned* prompted to   94 *My brother general* my fellows   95 (this line is unclear, and does not appear in the folio; the sense may be "the general grievance of the commonwealth joined with the nearer injury done [to his blood brother Scroop, executed by Henry IV] make this my own quarrel")   102 *unequal* unjust   104 *Construe* rate according to   110–11 *Were . . . signories* i.e., were not all the properties restored to you

That need to be revived and breathed in me?   114
The king that loved him, as the state stood then,
Was force perforce compelled to banish him.   116
And then that Henry Bolingbroke and he,
Being mounted and both rousèd in their seats,   118
Their neighing coursers daring of the spur,   119
Their armèd staves in charge, their beavers down,   120
Their eyes of fire sparkling through sights of steel,
And the loud trumpet blowing them together,
Then, then, when there was nothing could have stayed
My father from the breast of Bolingbroke,
O, when the king did throw his warder down,   125
His own life hung upon the staff he threw.
Then threw he down himself and all their lives
That by indictment and by dint of sword
Have since miscarried under Bolingbroke.

WESTMORELAND
You speak, Lord Mowbray, now you know not what.   *130*
The Earl of Hereford was reputed then   131
In England the most valiant gentleman.
Who knows on whom fortune would then have smiled?
But if your father had been victor there,
He ne'er had borne it out of Coventry.   135
For all the country in a general voice
Cried hate upon him, and all their prayers and love
Were set on Hereford, whom they doted on
And blessed and graced indeed, more than the king.]
But this is mere digression from my purpose.   *140*

---

114 *breathed* animated   116 *force perforce* i.e., willy-nilly (Richard II banished Mowbray's father for his complicity in Richard's uncle Gloucester's death, on account of which Bolingbroke challenged him to a duel)   118 *seats* saddles   119 *coursers* war horses; *daring of the spur* daring the spur to urge them on   120 *staves in charge* lances ready for action; *beavers* helmet visors   125 *warder* staff (Richard interrupted the duel, exiling both Mowbray and Bolingbroke; the latter returned after his father's death and eventually deposed Richard II to become Henry IV)   131 *Hereford* i.e., Bolingbroke   135 *it* i.e., the prize; *Coventry* (the site of combat)

Here come I from our princely general
To know your griefs, to tell you from his grace
That he will give you audience, and wherein
It shall appear that your demands are just,
145 You shall enjoy them, everything set off
That might so much as think you enemies.

MOWBRAY
But he hath forced us to compel this offer,
148 And it proceeds from policy, not love.

WESTMORELAND
149 Mowbray, you overween to take it so.
150 This offer comes from mercy, not from fear.
151 For, lo! within a ken our army lies,
Upon mine honor, all too confident
To give admittance to a thought of fear.
154 Our battle is more full of names than yours,
Our men more perfect in the use of arms,
Our armor all as strong, our cause the best.
157 Then reason will our hearts should be as good.
Say you not then our offer is compelled.

MOWBRAY
Well, by my will we shall admit no parley.

WESTMORELAND
160 That argues but the shame of your offense.
161 A rotten case abides no handling.

HASTINGS
Hath the Prince John a full commission,
163 In very ample virtue of his father,
To hear and absolutely to determine
165 Of what conditions we shall stand upon?

---

145 *set off* removed   148 *policy* strategic statecraft   149 *overween* are presumptuous   151 *ken* visible distance   154 *names* i.e., distinguished fighters of renown   157 *reason will* i.e., it is reasonable that   161 *rotten* weak; *abides* tolerates, withstands   163 *In . . . virtue* by full authority   165 *stand* insist

WESTMORELAND
   That is intended in the general's name.   166
   I muse you make so slight a question.   167
ARCHBISHOP
   Then take, my Lord of Westmoreland, this schedule,
   For this contains our general grievances.
   Each several article herein redressed,   *170*
   All members of our cause, both here and hence,
   That are insinewed to this action,   172
   Acquitted by a true substantial form   173
   And present execution of our wills   174
   To us and to our purposes confined,
   We come within our awful banks again   176
   And knit our powers to the arm of peace.
WESTMORELAND
   This will I show the general. Please you, lords,
   In sight of both our battles we may meet,   179
   And either end in peace – which God so frame –   *180*
   Or to the place of difference call the swords
   Which must decide it.
ARCHBISHOP   My lord, we will do so.
                             Exit Westmoreland.
MOWBRAY
   There is a thing within my bosom tells me
   That no conditions of our peace can stand.   184
HASTINGS
   Fear you not that. If we can make our peace
   Upon such large terms and so absolute   186
   As our conditions shall consist upon,   187
   Our peace shall stand as firm as rocky mountains.

---

166 *intended* implied, conveyed   167 *muse* wonder   172 *insinewed* joined
as by strong sinews   173 *substantial form* formal agreement   174
present . . . wills immediate satisfaction of our requests   176 *banks* i.e., as of
an overcharged river   179 *battles* armies   184 *stand* find acceptance, perse-
vere   186 *large* demanding   187 *consist* insist

MOWBRAY

189 Yea, but our valuation shall be such
190 That every slight and false-derivèd cause,
191 Yea, every idle, nice, and wanton reason
192 Shall to the king taste of this action,
193 That, were our royal faiths martyrs in love,
     We shall be winnowed with so rough a wind
     That even our corn shall seem as light as chaff
196 And good from bad find no partition.

ARCHBISHOP

     No, no, my lord. Note this. The king is weary
198 Of dainty and such picking grievances.
199 For he hath found to end one doubt by death
200 Revives two greater in the heirs of life,
201 And therefore will he wipe his tables clean
     And keep no telltale to his memory
     That may repeat and history his loss
     To new remembrance. For full well he knows
205 He cannot so precisely weed this land
206 As his misdoubts present occasion.
     His foes are so enrooted with his friends
     That, plucking to unfix an enemy,
     He doth unfasten so and shake a friend.
210 So that this land, like an offensive wife
211 That hath enraged him on to offer strokes,
     As he is striking, holds his infant up
213 And hangs resolved correction in the arm
     That was upreared to execution.

HASTINGS

215 Besides, the king hath wasted all his rods

---

189 *valuation* worth (in the king's eyes) **191** *nice* petty; *wanton* frivolous **192** *taste* remind, savor **193** *That . . . love* so that even if we suffered martyrdom for our love of the king **196** *partition* distinction **198** *dainty* precise; *picking* trifling **199** *doubt* danger, suspicion of threat **201** *tables* account books **205** *precisely* minutely, thoroughly **206** *misdoubts* suspicions **211** *him . . . strokes* him to beat her **213–14** *hangs . . . execution* causes him to halt his intended punishment **215** *rods* whipping rods

On late offenders, that he now doth lack
The very instruments of chastisement.
So that his power, like to a fangless lion,
May offer, but not hold.   219
ARCHBISHOP   'Tis very true.
And therefore be assured, my good lord marshal,   *220*
If we do now make our atonement well,   221
Our peace will, like a broken limb united,
Grow stronger for the breaking.
MOWBRAY   Be it so.
Here is returned my Lord of Westmoreland.
   Enter Westmoreland.
WESTMORELAND
The prince is here at hand. Pleaseth your lordship
To meet his grace just distance 'tween our armies.   226
MOWBRAY
Your grace of York, in God's name then, set forward.
ARCHBISHOP
Before, and greet his grace, my lord; we come.   228

                     *

∾ **IV.2** *Enter Prince John [of Lancaster] and his army.*

LANCASTER
You are well encountered here, my cousin Mowbray.
Good day to you, gentle lord archbishop.
And so to you, Lord Hastings, and to all.
My Lord of York, it better showed with you   4
When that your flock, assembled by the bell,
Encircled you to hear with reverence
Your exposition on the holy text

---

219 *offer* menace   **221** *atonement* repentance, reconciliation   **226** *just* even
228 *Before* go before
   IV.2 (It is not clear that any change of scene was intended here. In the
quarto the stage direction follows l. 226; in the folio, after l. 228. The location remains, in any case, similar to the previous scene.)   **4** *showed with* become

8 Than now to see you here an iron man,
 Cheering a rout of rebels with your drum,
10 Turning the word to sword and life to death.
 That man that sits within a monarch's heart
 And ripens in the sunshine of his favor,
13 Would he abuse the countenance of the king,
 Alack, what mischiefs might he set abroach
 In shadow of such greatness. With you, lord bishop,
 It is even so. Who hath not heard it spoken
 How deep you were within the books of God?
 To us the speaker in His parliament,
 To us the imagined voice of God himself,
20 The very opener and intelligencer
 Between the grace, the sanctities of heaven
22 And our dull workings. O, who shall believe
23 But you misuse the reverence of your place,
 Employ the countenance and grace of heaven,
25 As a false favorite doth his prince's name,
26 In deeds dishonorable? You have ta'en up,
 Under the counterfeited zeal of God,
28 The subjects of His substitute, my father,
 And both against the peace of heaven and him
30 Have here upswarmed them.
ARCHBISHOP   Good my Lord of Lancaster
 I am not here against your father's peace,
 But, as I told my Lord of Westmoreland,
33 The time misordered doth, in common sense,
 Crowd us and crush us to this monstrous form,
35 To hold our safety up. I sent your grace
36 The parcels and particulars of our grief,
 The which hath been with scorn shoved from the court,

---

8 *iron man* armor-clad man of war 10 *word* scripture 13 *Would he* if he
were to; *countenance* favor 20 *opener* interpreter; *intelligencer* messenger, spy,
revealer 22 *workings* perceptions, senses 23 *But* but that 25 *favorite* i.e.,
of the king 26 *ta'en up* enlisted 28 *substitute* i.e., on earth, the king 33
time misordered current disorders; *in common sense* as all can see 35 *hold*
maintain 36 *parcels* details

Whereon this Hydra son of war is born,   38
Whose dangerous eyes may well be charmed asleep   39
With grant of our most just and right desires,   40
And true obedience, of this madness cured,
Stoop tamely to the foot of majesty.
MOWBRAY
    If not, we ready are to try our fortunes
    To the last man.
HASTINGS   And though we here fall down,
    We have supplies to second our attempt.   45
    If they miscarry, theirs shall second them,
    And so success of mischief shall be born   47
    And heir from heir shall hold this quarrel up
    Whiles England shall have generation.   49
LANCASTER
    You are too shallow, Hastings, much too shallow,   50
    To sound the bottom of the after-times.   51
WESTMORELAND
    Pleaseth your grace to answer them directly
    How far forth you do like their articles.
LANCASTER
    I like them all, and do allow them well,
    And swear here, by the honor of my blood,
    My father's purposes have been mistook,
    And some about him have too lavishly   57
    Wrested his meaning and authority.   58
    My lord, these griefs shall be with speed redressed,
    Upon my soul, they shall. If this may please you,   60
    Discharge your powers unto their several counties,
    As we will ours. And here between the armies
    Let's drink together friendly and embrace,

---

38 *Hydra* i.e., many-headed monster 39 *eyes* e.g., of Argus (here linked with the Hydra), Juno's 100-eyed guard, who was charmed asleep by Mercury's music 45 *supplies* reinforcements; *second* back up 47 *success* succession 49 *generation* offspring 51 *sound the bottom* predict the outcome 57 *some* i.e., certain courtiers; *lavishly* freely 58 *Wrested* twisted

That all their eyes may bear those tokens home
Of our restorèd love and amity.

ARCHBISHOP
I take your princely word for these redresses.

[LANCASTER]
I give it you, and will maintain my word.
And thereupon I drink unto your grace.

[HASTINGS]
Go, captain, and deliver to the army
70   This news of peace. Let them have pay, and part.
71   I know it will well please them. Hie thee, captain.
                                           Exit [Officer].

ARCHBISHOP
To you, my noble Lord of Westmoreland.

WESTMORELAND
I pledge your grace, and, if you knew what pains
74   I have bestowed to breed this present peace,
You would drink freely. But my love to ye
Shall show itself more openly hereafter.

ARCHBISHOP
I do not doubt you.

WESTMORELAND   I am glad of it.
Health to my lord and gentle cousin, Mowbray.

MOWBRAY
You wish me health in very happy season,
80   For I am, on the sudden, something ill.

ARCHBISHOP
81   Against ill chances men are ever merry,
82   But heaviness foreruns the good event.

WESTMORELAND
Therefore be merry, coz, since sudden sorrow
Serves to say thus, "Some good thing comes tomorrow."

---

71 *Hie* hurry   74 *bestowed* taken   80 *on* all of a; *something* somewhat   81
Against in anticipation of   82 *heaviness foreruns* sadness precedes

ARCHBISHOP
  Believe me, I am passing light in spirit.   85
MOWBRAY
  So much the worse, if your own rule be true.
    Shouts [within].
LANCASTER
  The word of peace is rendered. Hark, how they shout!   87
MOWBRAY
  This had been cheerful after victory.   88
ARCHBISHOP
  A peace is of the nature of a conquest,
  For then both parties nobly are subdued,   90
  And neither party loser.
LANCASTER   Go, my lord,
  And let our army be dischargèd too.
                           [Exit Westmoreland.]
  And, good my lord, so please you, let our trains   93
  March by us, that we may peruse the men
  We should have coped withal.   95
ARCHBISHOP   Go, good Lord Hastings,
  And, ere they be dismissed, let them march by.
                            [Exit Hastings.]
LANCASTER
  I trust, lords, we shall lie tonight together.
    Enter Westmoreland.
  Now cousin, wherefore stands our army still?   98
WESTMORELAND
  The leaders, having charge from you to stand,   99
  Will not go off until they hear you speak.   *100*
LANCASTER
  They know their duties.

---

85 *passing* exceedingly   87 *rendered* proclaimed   88 *had been* would have
been   93 *trains* armies   95 *coped withal* engaged in battle   98 *wherefore*
why   99 *charge* orders

Enter Hastings.

HASTINGS
My lord, our army is dispersed already.
Like youthful steers unyoked, they take their courses
East, west, north, south, or, like a school broke up,
105   Each hurries toward his home and sporting-place.

WESTMORELAND
Good tidings, my Lord Hastings, for the which
I do arrest thee, traitor, of high treason.
And you, lord archbishop, and you, Lord Mowbray,
109   Of capital treason I attach you both.

MOWBRAY
110   Is this proceeding just and honorable?

WESTMORELAND
Is your assembly so?

ARCHBISHOP
112   Will you thus break your faith?

LANCASTER   I pawned thee none.
I promised you redress of these same grievances
Whereof you did complain, which, by mine honor,
I will perform with a most Christian care.
116   But for you, rebels, look to taste the due
117   Meet for rebellion and such acts as yours.
118   Most shallowly did you these arms commence,
119   Fondly brought here and foolishly sent hence.
120   Strike up our drums, pursue the scattered stray.
God, and not we, hath safely fought today.
122   Some guard these traitors to the block of death,
Treason's true bed and yielder up of breath.

                                        [Exeunt.]

                    *

---

105 *sporting-place* playground 109 *capital* punishable by death; *attach* charge, arrest 112 *pawned* promised, pledged 116 *due* reward 117 *Meet for* suited to 118 *arms* armed hostilities 119 *Fondly* foolishly 120 *stray* stragglers 122 *Some* someone

∾ **IV.3** *Alarum. Excursions. Enter Falstaff [and Coleville, meeting].*

FALSTAFF   What's your name, sir? Of what condition are 1
you, and of what place, I pray?

COLEVILLE   I am a knight, sir, and my name is Coleville
of the dale.   4

FALSTAFF   Well, then, Coleville is your name, a knight is
your degree, and your place the dale. Coleville shall be
still your name, a traitor your degree, and the dungeon
your place, a place deep enough. So shall you be still
Coleville of the dale.

COLEVILLE   Are not you Sir John Falstaff?   10

FALSTAFF   As good a man as he, sir, whoe'er I am. Do ye
yield, sir, or shall I sweat for you? If I do sweat, they are 12
the drops of thy lovers, and they weep for thy death. 13
Therefore rouse up fear and trembling, and do observ- 14
ance to my mercy.

COLEVILLE   I think you are Sir John Falstaff, and in that
thought yield me.

FALSTAFF   I have a whole school of tongues in this belly 18
of mine, and not a tongue of them all speaks any other
word but my name. An I had but a belly of any indif- 20
ferency, I were simply the most active fellow in Europe.
My womb, my womb, my womb undoes me. Here 22
comes our general.

Enter [Prince] John [of Lancaster], Westmoreland,
[Blunt,] and the rest. Retreat [sounded].

LANCASTER
The heat is past, follow no further now.   24
Call in the powers, good cousin Westmoreland.

IV.3 The battlefield **1** *condition* rank **4** *dale* valley **12** *sweat for* force
13 *drops* tears; *lovers* friends **14–15** *observance* reverence **18–20** *school . . .
name* i.e., my (big) belly proclaims my identity **20–21** *indifferency* moder-
ation **22** *womb* belly; *undoes me* gives me away, blows my cover **24** *heat*
race (to catch rebel stragglers)

[Exit Westmoreland.]
Now, Falstaff, where have you been all this while?
When everything is ended, then you come.
These tardy tricks of yours will, on my life,
One time or other break some gallows' back.

30 FALSTAFF I would be sorry, my lord, but it should be
thus. I never knew yet but rebuke and check was the reward of valor. Do you think me a swallow, an arrow, or a
33 bullet? Have I, in my poor and old motion, the expedi-
34 tion of thought? I have speeded hither with the very ex-
35 tremest inch of possibility. I have foundered nine score
36 and odd posts, and here, travel-tainted as I am, have, in
my pure and immaculate valor, taken Sir John Coleville
of the dale, a most furious knight and valorous enemy.
But what of that? He saw me, and yielded, that I may
40 justly say, with the hook-nosed fellow of Rome, their
Caesar, "I came, saw, and overcame."

LANCASTER It was more of his courtesy than your de-
serving.

FALSTAFF I know not. Here he is, and here I yield him.
45 And I beseech your grace, let it be booked with the rest
of this day's deeds, or, by the Lord, I will have it in a
47 particular ballad else, with mine own picture on the top
on't, Coleville kissing my foot. To the which course if I
49 be enforced, if you do not all show like gilt twopences
50 to me, and I in the clear sky of fame o'ershine you as
51 much as the full moon doth the cinders of the element,
which show like pins' heads to her, believe not the word
53 of the noble. Therefore let me have right, and let desert
54 mount.

LANCASTER Thine's too heavy to mount.

---

33 *motion* agility, movement 33–34 *expedition* speed 34–35 *very . . . possibility* as quickly as possible 35 *foundered* lamed 36 *posts* post-horses 40
hook-nosed . . . Rome i.e., Julius Caesar 45 *booked* recorded 47 *particular
ballad* special ballad published for the occasion 49 *show* look; *gilt twopences*
coins gilded to appear like coins of greater value 50 *to* compared to 51
cinders of the element stars 53 *desert* worth 54 *mount* rise, be promoted

FALSTAFF   Let it shine, then.

LANCASTER   Thine's too thick to shine.

FALSTAFF   Let it do something, my good lord, that may
do me good, and call it what you will.

LANCASTER   Is thy name Coleville?   60

COLEVILLE   It is, my lord.

LANCASTER   A famous rebel art thou, Coleville.

FALSTAFF   And a famous true subject took him.

COLEVILLE
I am, my lord, but as my betters are
That led me hither. Had they been ruled by me,
You should have won them dearer than you have.   66

FALSTAFF   I know not how they sold themselves. But
thou, like a kind fellow, gavest thyself away gratis, and I   68
thank thee for thee.
          Enter Westmoreland.

LANCASTER
Now, have you left pursuit?   70

WESTMORELAND
Retreat is made and execution stayed.   71

LANCASTER
Send Coleville with his confederates
To York, to present execution.   73
Blunt, lead him hence, and see you guard him sure.   74
          [Exeunt Blunt and others with Coleville.]
And now dispatch we toward the court, my lords.   75
I hear the king my father is sore sick.   76
Our news shall go before us to his majesty,
Which, cousin, you shall bear to comfort him,   78
And we with sober speed will follow you.

FALSTAFF
My lord, I beseech you give me leave to go   80

---

66 *dearer* in a more costly fashion (i.e., through battle)   68 *gratis* free   71
Retreat . . . stayed the order for retreat has been delivered and that for execution withdrawn   73 *present* immediate   74 *sure* securely   75 *dispatch we* let
us hurry   76 *sore* very   78 *cousin* i.e., Westmoreland

81 Through Gloucestershire. And when you come to
    court,
82 Stand my good lord, pray, in your good report.
    LANCASTER
83 Fare you well, Falstaff. I, in my condition,
    Shall better speak of you than you deserve.
                          [Exeunt all but Falstaff.]
85 FALSTAFF I would you had but the wit. 'Twere better
    than your dukedom. Good faith, this same young sober-
    blooded boy doth not love me, nor a man cannot make
    him laugh. But that's no marvel, he drinks no wine.
89 There's never none of these demure boys come to any
90 proof, for thin drink doth so overcool their blood, and
91 making many fish-meals, that they fall into a kind of
92 male greensickness, and then, when they marry, they
93 get wenches. They are generally fools and cowards,
94 which some of us should be too, but for inflammation.
95 A good sherris-sack hath a twofold operation in it. It
96 ascends me into the brain, dries me there all the foolish
97 and dull and crudy vapors which environ it, makes it
98 apprehensive, quick, forgetive, full of nimble, fiery, and
    delectable shapes, which, delivered o'er to the voice,
100 the tongue, which is the birth, becomes excellent wit.
    The second property of your excellent sherris is the
    warming of the blood, which, before cold and settled,
103 left the liver white and pale, which is the badge of
    pusillanimity and cowardice. But the sherris warms it
105 and makes it course from the inwards to the parts

---

81 *Through* via   82 *Stand . . . lord* be my patron   83 *in my condition* i.e., as
a commander   85 *'Twere better* it would be worth more (to be so witty)
89–90 *come . . . proof* arrive at any test   90 *thin drink* weak beer   91 *fish-
meals* i.e., not hearty meat   92 *greensickness* anemia, associated with young
girls   93 *get* beget, breed, father   94 *inflammation* intoxication   95 *sherris-
sack* sherry   96 *ascends me into* i.e., ascends into my   97 *crudy* curded; *environ* surround   98 *forgetive* inventive   100 *wit* mental power   103 *liver*
(regarded as the seat of courage)   105 *course* run   105–106 *parts extremes*
extremities

extremes. It illumineth the face, which as a beacon
gives warning to all the rest of this little kingdom, man,
to arm, and then the vital commoners and inland petty   108
spirits muster me all to their captain, the heart, who,
great and puffed up with this retinue, doth any deed of   *110*
courage, and this valor comes of sherris. So that skill in
the weapon is nothing without sack, for that sets it   112
a-work, and learning a mere hoard of gold kept by a   113
devil, till sack commences it and sets it in act and use.   114
Hereof comes it that Prince Harry is valiant, for the cold
blood he did naturally inherit of his father, he hath, like
lean, sterile, and bare land, manured, husbanded, and   117
tilled with excellent endeavor of drinking good and
good store of fertile sherris, that he is become very hot
and valiant. If I had a thousand sons, the first humane   *120*
principle I would teach them should be to forswear
thin potations and to addict themselves to sack.

    Enter Bardolph.

How now, Bardolph?

BARDOLPH   The army is discharged all and gone.

FALSTAFF   Let them go. I'll through Gloucestershire, and
there will I visit Master Robert Shallow, esquire. I have   126
him already tempering between my finger and my
thumb, and shortly will I seal with him. Come away.   128

                            [Exeunt.]

              *

108–9 *vital . . . spirits* inward forces   112 *it* i.e., the weapon   113 *a* is a
114 *commences it* inaugurates its action (as in a university commencement)
117 *husbanded* farmed   126–28 *I . . . thumb* I am even now warming him
(into sealing wax)   128 *seal with* make use of; close a bargain with

∾ **IV.4** *Enter the King, Warwick, Thomas Duke of*
Clarence, Humphrey [Duke] of Gloucester [, and
others].

KING
    Now, lords, if God doth give successful end
2   To this debate that bleedeth at our doors,
3   We will our youth lead on to higher fields
4   And draw no swords but what are sanctified.
5   Our navy is addressed, our power collected,
6   Our substitutes in absence well invested,
7   And everything lies level to our wish.
    Only, we want a little personal strength,
    And pause us, till these rebels, now afoot,
10 Come underneath the yoke of government.
WARWICK
    Both which we doubt not but your majesty
    Shall soon enjoy.
KING   Humphrey, my son of Gloucester,
    Where is the prince your brother?
GLOUCESTER
    I think he's gone to hunt, my lord, at Windsor.
KING
    And how accompanied?
GLOUCESTER   I do not know, my lord.
KING
    Is not his brother, Thomas of Clarence, with him?
GLOUCESTER
17 No, my good lord, he is in presence here.
CLARENCE
    What would my lord and father?

IV.4 Within King Henry's palace **2** *debate* quarrel **3** *higher* i.e., the Holy
Land **4** *what* those that; *sanctified* i.e., in and by a religious crusade
5 *addressed* ready **6** *substitutes* deputies **7** *level to* in accordance with **17**
in presence present at court

KING
    Nothing but well to thee, Thomas of Clarence.
    How chance thou art not with the prince thy brother?   *20*
    He loves thee, and thou dost neglect him, Thomas;
    Thou hast a better place in his affection
    Than all thy brothers. Cherish it, my boy,
    And noble offices thou mayst effect   *24*
    Of mediation, after I am dead,
    Between his greatness and thy other brethren.
    Therefore omit him not, blunt not his love,   *27*
    Nor lose the good advantage of his grace
    By seeming cold or careless of his will.
    For he is gracious, if he be observed.   *30*
    He hath a tear for pity and a hand
    Open as day for meting charity.   *32*
    Yet notwithstanding, being incensed, he's flint,
    As humorous as winter and as sudden   *34*
    As flaws congealèd in the spring of day.   *35*
    His temper, therefore, must be well observed.
    Chide him for faults, and do it reverently,
    When you perceive his blood inclined to mirth,
    But, being moody, give him time and scope,
    Till that his passions, like a whale on ground,   *40*
    Confound themselves with working. Learn this,   *41*
     Thomas,
    And thou shalt prove a shelter to thy friends,
    A hoop of gold to bind thy brothers in,
    That the united vessel of their blood,
    Mingled with venom of suggestion –   *45*
    As, force perforce, the age will pour it in –   *46*
    Shall never leak, though it do work as strong
    As aconitum or rash gunpowder.   *48*

---

24 *offices* functions   27 *omit* neglect   30 *observed* respected   32 *meting* distributing   34 *humorous* moody   35 *flaws* snowflakes   41 *Confound* consume; *working* struggling   45 *suggestion* suspicion, insinuation   46 *force perforce* necessarily   48 *aconitum* a strong poison derived from the plant monkshood

CLARENCE
    I shall observe him with all care and love.
KING
50   Why art thou not at Windsor with him, Thomas?
CLARENCE
    He is not there today; he dines in London.
KING
    And how accompanied? Canst thou tell that?
CLARENCE
53   With Poins and other his continual followers.
KING
54   Most subject is the fattest soil to weeds,
    And he, the noble image of my youth,
    Is overspread with them. Therefore my grief
    Stretches itself beyond the hour of death.
    The blood weeps from my heart when I do shape
59   In forms imaginary the unguided days
60   And rotten times that you shall look upon
    When I am sleeping with my ancestors.
    For when his headstrong riot hath no curb,
    When rage and hot blood are his counselors,
64   When means and lavish manners meet together,
    O, with what wings shall his affections fly
66   Towards fronting peril and opposed decay!
WARWICK
67   My gracious lord, you look beyond him quite.
    The prince but studies his companions
69   Like a strange tongue, wherein, to gain the language,
70   'Tis needful that the most immodest word
    Be looked upon and learned, which once attained,
    Your highness knows, comes to no further use
73   But to be known and hated. So, like gross terms,

---

53 *continual* usual   54 *fattest* richest   59 *unguided* ungoverned   64 *lavish* licentious, willful   66 *fronting . . . decay* danger and ruin that lie before him   67 *look beyond* misunderstand   69 *strange* foreign   73 *gross terms* coarse language

The prince will in the perfectness of time   74
Cast off his followers, and their memory
Shall as a pattern or a measure live,
By which his grace must mete the lives of others,   77
Turning past evils to advantages.

KING
'Tis seldom when the bee doth leave her comb   79
In the dead carrion.   80
    Enter Westmoreland.
              Who's here? Westmoreland?

WESTMORELAND
Health to my sovereign, and new happiness
Added to that that I am to deliver.
Prince John your son doth kiss your grace's hand.
Mowbray, the Bishop Scroop, Hastings and all
Are brought to the correction of your law.
There is not now a rebel's sword unsheathed,
But Peace puts forth her olive everywhere.   87
The manner how this action hath been borne
Here at more leisure may your highness read,
With every course in his particular.   90

KING
O Westmoreland, thou art a summer bird,   91
Which ever in the haunch of winter sings   92
The lifting up of day.
    Enter Harcourt.
              Look, here's more news.

HARCOURT
From enemies heaven keep your majesty,
And, when they stand against you, may they fall
As those that I am come to tell you of!
The Earl Northumberland and the Lord Bardolph,

---

74 *perfectness* perfection   77 *mete* appraise, judge   79–80 *'Tis . . . carrion* it
is rare that the bee abandons its comb in a carcass – i.e., the Prince is unlikely
to leave his current haunts   87 *olive* olive branch, sign of peace   92 *haunch*
latter end

With a great power of English and of Scots,
99   Are by the shrieve of Yorkshire overthrown.
100 The manner and true order of the fight
This packet, please it you, contains at large.

KING
And wherefore should these good news make me sick?
Will Fortune never come with both hands full,
104 But write her fair words still in foulest letters?
She either gives a stomach and no food –
Such are the poor, in health – or else a feast
107 And takes away the stomach – such are the rich,
That have abundance and enjoy it not.
I should rejoice now at this happy news,
110 And now my sight fails, and my brain is giddy.
O me! Come near me. Now I am much ill.

GLOUCESTER
Comfort, your majesty!

CLARENCE   O my royal father!

WESTMORELAND
My sovereign lord, cheer up yourself, look up.

WARWICK
Be patient, princes. You do know these fits
115 Are with his highness very ordinary.
116 Stand from him, give him air, he'll straight be well.

CLARENCE
117 No, no, he cannot long hold out these pangs.
The incessant care and labor of his mind
119 Hath wrought the mure that should confine it in
120 So thin that life looks through and will break out.

GLOUCESTER
121 The people fear me, for they do observe
122 Unfathered heirs and loathly births of nature.

---

99 *shrieve* sheriff 104 *still* yet, ever 107 *stomach* appetite 115 *ordinary* usual 116 *straight* shortly 117 *hold out* withstand, suffer 119 *mure* wall; *it* i.e., life 121 *fear* frighten 122 *Unfathered heirs* persons thought to be supernaturally conceived; *loathly births* deformed infants

The seasons change their manners, as the year
Had found some months asleep and leaped them over.

CLARENCE
The river hath thrice flowed, no ebb between,   125
And the old folk, time's doting chronicles,   126
Say it did so a little time before
That our great-grandsire, Edward, sicked and died.   128

WARWICK
Speak lower, princes, for the king recovers.

GLOUCESTER
This apoplexy will certain be his end.   130

KING
I pray you, take me up, and bear me hence
Into some other chamber. Softly, pray.
    [They bear him to another place.]
                        ✳

❧ **IV.5**

[KING]
Let there be no noise made, my gentle friends,
Unless some dull and favorable hand   2
Will whisper music to my weary spirit.

WARWICK
Call for the music in the other room.

KING
Set me the crown upon my pillow here.

CLARENCE
His eye is hollow, and he changes much.   6

WARWICK
Less noise, less noise!
    Enter Prince Henry.

PRINCE   Who saw the Duke of Clarence?

---

125 *river* the Thames; *ebb* ebb tide   126 *chronicles* historians, records   128
Edward Edward III; *sicked* sickened
    IV.5 2 *dull* soothing; *favorable* kindly, gentle   6 *changes* grows pale

CLARENCE
8   I am here, brother, full of heaviness.
PRINCE
9   How now! Rain within doors, and none abroad!
10   How doth the king?
GLOUCESTER
     Exceeding ill.
PRINCE   Heard he the good news yet?
     Tell it him.
GLOUCESTER
     He altered much upon the hearing it.
PRINCE
14   If he be sick with joy, he'll recover without physic.
WARWICK
     Not so much noise, my lords. Sweet prince, speak low.
     The king your father is disposed to sleep.
CLARENCE
     Let us withdraw into the other room.
WARWICK
     Will't please your grace to go along with us?
PRINCE
     No, I will sit and watch here by the king.
                              [Exeunt all but the Prince.]
20   Why doth the crown lie there upon his pillow,
     Being so troublesome a bedfellow?
22   O polished perturbation! Golden care!
23   That keep'st the ports of slumber open wide
     To many a watchful night! Sleep with it now!
     Yet not so sound and half so deeply sweet
26   As he whose brow with homely biggen bound
     Snores out the watch of night. O majesty!
     When thou dost pinch thy bearer, thou dost sit
     Like a rich armor worn in heat of day,

---

8 *heaviness* sadness   9 *Rain* i.e., tears   14 *physic* medical attention   22 *per-turbation* cause of unease   23 *ports of slumber* i.e., eyes   26 *biggen* nightcap

That scald'st with safety. By his gates of breath   30
There lies a downy feather which stirs not.
Did he suspire, that light and weightless down   32
Perforce must move. My gracious lord! my father!
This sleep is sound indeed. This is a sleep
That from this golden rigol hath divorced   35
So many English kings. Thy due from me
Is tears and heavy sorrows of the blood,
Which nature, love, and filial tenderness
Shall, O dear father, pay thee plenteously.
My due from thee is this imperial crown,   40
Which, as immediate from thy place and blood,   41
Derives itself to me. *[Puts on the crown.]* Lo, where it sits, 42
Which God shall guard. And put the world's whole
    strength
Into one giant arm, it shall not force
This lineal honor from me. This from thee   45
Will I to mine leave, as 'tis left to me.   *[Exit.]*
KING
    Warwick! Gloucester! Clarence!
        Enter Warwick, Gloucester, Clarence.
CLARENCE
    Doth the king call?
WARWICK
    What would your majesty? How fares your grace?
KING
    Why did you leave me here alone, my lords?   50
CLARENCE
    We left the prince my brother here, my liege,
    Who undertook to sit and watch by you.
KING
    The Prince of Wales! Where is he? Let me see him.
    He is not here.

---

30 *scald'st with safety* burns while it protects 32 *suspire* breathe 35 *rigol*
circle – i.e., the crown 41 *immediate from* nearest to 42 *Derives* descends
45 *lineal* inherited

WARWICK
> The door is open; he is gone this way.

GLOUCESTER
> He came not through the chamber where we stayed.

KING
> Where is the crown? Who took it from my pillow?

WARWICK
> When we withdrew, my liege, we left it here.

KING
> The prince hath ta'en it hence. Go, seek him out.

60 > Is he so hasty that he doth suppose
> My sleep my death?
> Find him, my Lord of Warwick, chide him hither.
> > *[Exit Warwick.]*

63 > This part of his conjoins with my disease
> And helps to end me. See, sons, what things you are!
> How quickly nature falls into revolt
> When gold becomes her object!
> For this the foolish overcareful fathers

68 > Have broke their sleep with thoughts, their brains with
> > care,
> Their bones with industry.

70 > For this they have engrossed and pilèd up
71 > The cankered heaps of strange-achievèd gold;
72 > For this they have been thoughtful to invest
> Their sons with arts and martial exercises.

74 > When, like the bee, tolling from every flower
> [The virtuous sweets],
> Our thighs packed with wax, our mouths with honey,
> We bring it to the hive, and, like the bees,

78 > Are murdered for our pains. This bitter taste
> Yields his engrossments to the ending father.

---

60 *hasty* eager 63 *part* behavior 68 *thoughts* worries 70 *engrossed* accumulated 71 *cankered* rusting, tarnished; *strange-achievèd* hard-won, by unusual means 72 *invest* instruct 74 *tolling* gathering 78–79 *This . . . father* the dying father's efforts give him this bitter taste

Enter Warwick.
Now, where is he that will not stay so long   80
Till his friend sickness hath determined me?   81
WARWICK
My lord, I found the prince in the next room,
Washing with kindly tears his gentle cheeks,   83
With such a deep demeanor in great sorrow   84
That tyranny, which never quaffed but blood,   85
Would, by beholding him, have washed his knife
With gentle eye-drops. He is coming hither.   87
KING
But wherefore did he take away the crown?
    Enter [Prince] Henry.
Lo, where he comes. Come hither to me, Harry.
Depart the chamber, leave us here alone.   90
                          Exeunt [Warwick and the rest].
PRINCE
I never thought to hear you speak again.
KING
Thy wish was father, Harry, to that thought.
I stay too long by thee, I weary thee.
Dost thou so hunger for mine empty chair
That thou wilt needs invest thee with my honors
Before thy hour be ripe? O foolish youth!
Thou seek'st the greatness that will overwhelm thee.
Stay but a little, for my cloud of dignity   98
Is held from falling with so weak a wind
That it will quickly drop. My day is dim.   100
Thou hast stolen that which after some few hours
Were thine without offense, and at my death
Thou hast sealed up my expectation.   103
Thy life did manifest thou lovedst me not,
And thou wilt have me die assured of it.

---

81 *determined* finished   83 *kindly* natural   84 *deep* intense   85 *quaffed but* drank anything except   87 *eye-drops* tears   98 *Stay* wait   103 *sealed up* confirmed

Thou hidest a thousand daggers in thy thoughts,
Which thou hast whetted on thy stony heart,
To stab at half an hour of my life.
109 What! Canst thou not forbear me half an hour?
110 Then get thee gone and dig my grave thyself,
And bid the merry bells ring to thine ear
That thou art crownèd, not that I am dead.
Let all the tears that should bedew my hearse
114 Be drops of balm to sanctify thy head.
115 Only compound me with forgotten dust;
Give that which gave thee life unto the worms.
Pluck down my officers, break my decrees,
118 For now a time is come to mock at form.
Harry the Fifth is crowned. Up, vanity!
120 Down, royal state! All you sage counselors, hence!
And to the English court assemble now,
From every region, apes of idleness!
Now, neighbor confines, purge you of your scum.
Have you a ruffian that will swear, drink, dance,
Revel the night, rob, murder, and commit
The oldest sins the newest kind of ways?
Be happy, he will trouble you no more.
England shall double gild his treble guilt,
England shall give him office, honor, might,
130 For the fifth Harry from curbed license plucks
The muzzle of restraint, and the wild dog
132 Shall flesh his tooth on every innocent.
O my poor kingdom, sick with civil blows!
134 When that my care could not withhold thy riots,
135 What wilt thou do when riot is thy care?
O, thou wilt be a wilderness again,
Peopled with wolves, thy old inhabitants.

---

109 *forbear* spare, afford   114 *balm* consecrating oil   115 *compound* mingle   118 *form* ceremony, order   120 *state* ceremony   130 *curbed license* restrained riotousness   132 *flesh his tooth* bite (in order to acquire a taste for blood)   134 *care* order; *withhold* prevent   135 *care* concern

PRINCE
　　O, pardon me, my liege! But for my tears,　　　　　138
　　The moist impediments unto my speech,
　　I had forestalled this dear and deep rebuke　　　　140
　　Ere you with grief had spoke and I had heard
　　The course of it so far. There is your crown,
　　And He that wears the crown immortally
　　Long guard it yours. If I affect it more　　　　　144
　　Than as your honor and as your renown,
　　Let me no more from this obedience rise,　　　　146
　　Which my most inward true and duteous spirit
　　Teacheth, this prostrate and exterior bending.
　　God witness with me, when I here came in,
　　And found no course of breath within your majesty,　150
　　How cold it struck my heart. If I do feign,
　　O, let me in my present wildness die
　　And never live to show the incredulous world
　　The noble change that I have purposèd.　　　　154
　　Coming to look on you, thinking you dead,
　　And dead almost, my liege, to think you were,
　　I spake unto this crown as having sense,
　　And thus upbraided it: "The care on thee depending
　　Hath fed upon the body of my father.
　　Therefore, thou best of gold art worst of gold.　　160
　　Other, less fine in carat, is more precious,
　　Preserving life in medicine potable,　　　　　162
　　But thou, most fine, most honored, most renowned,
　　Hast eat thy bearer up." Thus, my most royal liege,
　　Accusing it, I put it on my head,
　　To try with it, as with an enemy　　　　　166
　　That had before my face murdered my father,
　　The quarrel of a true inheritor.
　　But if it did infect my blood with joy,

---

138 *But* were it not 140 *dear* severe 144 *affect* desire 146 *obedience*
obeisance (kneeling posture) 154 *purposèd* intended 162 *medicine potable*
soluble gold was often prescribed as a medicine 166 *try* struggle, combat

170 Or swell my thoughts to any strain of pride,
If any rebel or vain spirit of mine
Did with the least affection of a welcome
Give entertainment to the might of it,
Let God for ever keep it from my head
And make me as the poorest vassal is
That doth with awe and terror kneel to it.

KING
[O my son,]
God put it in thy mind to take it hence,
That thou mightst win the more thy father's love,
180 Pleading so wisely in excuse of it!
Come hither, Harry, sit thou by my bed,
182 And hear, I think, the very latest counsel
That ever I shall breathe. God knows, my son,
184 By what bypaths and indirect crooked ways
I met this crown, and I myself know well
How troublesome it sat upon my head.
187 To thee it shall descend with better quiet,
188 Better opinion, better confirmation,
189 For all the soil of the achievement goes
190 With me into the earth. It seemed in me
But as an honor snatched with boisterous hand,
And I had many living to upbraid
My gain of it by their assistances,
Which daily grew to quarrel and to bloodshed
195 Wounding supposèd peace. All these bold fears
Thou seest with peril I have answerèd,
For all my reign hath been but as a scene
Acting that argument. And now my death
199 Changes the mode, for what in me was purchased
200 Falls upon thee in a more fairer sort,

---

170 *strain* feeling   182 *latest* last   184 *bypaths . . . ways* i.e., in the deposition of Richard II   187 *quiet* peace   188 *opinion* reputation   189 *soil* stain   195 *bold fears* grave dangers   199 *mode* musical key, mood; *purchased* acquired by a transaction   200 *fairer sort* more graceful, proper way

So thou the garland wear'st successively.   201
Yet, though thou stand'st more sure than I could do,   202
Thou art not firm enough, since griefs are green.   203
And all my friends, which thou must make thy friends,
Have but their stings and teeth newly ta'en out,
By whose fell working I was first advanced   206
And by whose power I well might lodge a fear   207
To be again displaced. Which to avoid,
I cut them off, and had a purpose now
To lead out many to the Holy Land,   210
Lest rest and lying still might make them look
Too near unto my state. Therefore, my Harry,   212
Be it thy course to busy giddy minds   213
With foreign quarrels, that action, hence borne out,   214
May waste the memory of the former days.
More would I, but my lungs are wasted so   216
That strength of speech is utterly denied me.
How I came by the crown, O God forgive,
And grant it may with thee in true peace live!

PRINCE
  [My gracious liege,]   220
  You won it, wore it, kept it, gave it me.
  Then plain and right must my possession be,
  Which I with more than with a common pain   223
  'Gainst all the world will rightfully maintain.
        Enter [Prince John of] Lancaster [and Warwick].

KING
  Look, look, here comes my John of Lancaster.

LANCASTER
  Health, peace, and happiness to my royal father!

KING
  Thou bring'st me happiness and peace, son John,

---

201 *successively* by hereditary right 202 *sure* security 203 *griefs are green*
i.e., the tensions of civil unrest are fresh 206 *fell* fierce; *advanced* raised up
207 *lodge* harbor 212 *Too . . . state* closely into my power 213 *course* plan
214 *that* so that 216 *More would I* i.e., I'd say more 223 *pain* effort

But health, alack, with youthful wings is flown
From this bare withered trunk. Upon thy sight
230   My worldly business makes a period.
Where is my Lord of Warwick?

PRINCE   My Lord of Warwick!

KING
Doth any name particular belong
Unto the lodging where I first did swoon?

WARWICK
234   'Tis called Jerusalem, my noble lord.

KING
Laud be to God! Even there my life must end.
It hath been prophesied to me many years
I should not die but in Jerusalem,
Which vainly I supposed the Holy Land.
But bear me to that chamber; there I'll lie.
240   In that Jerusalem shall Harry die.   *[Exeunt.]*

*

∾ **V.1** *Enter Shallow, Falstaff, and Bardolph [and Page].*

1 SHALLOW By cock and pie, sir, you shall not away tonight. What, Davy, I say!

FALSTAFF You must excuse me, Master Robert Shallow.

SHALLOW I will not excuse you, you shall not be excused, excuses shall not be admitted, there is no excuse
shall serve, you shall not be excused. Why, Davy!
    Enter Davy.

DAVY Here, sir.

SHALLOW Davy, Davy, Davy, Davy, let me see, Davy.
9 Let me see, Davy, let me see. Yea, marry, William cook,

---

230 *period* i.e., end 234 *Jerusalem* (actually in Westminster Abbey)
  V.1 Shallow's house in Gloucestershire 1 *By cock and pie* (a mild oath
meaning "By God and the book," meaning the book of the Roman Catholic
Church containing the ordering of Church offices) 9 *William cook* William
the cook

bid him come hither. Sir John, you shall not be ex- 10
cused.

DAVY Marry, sir, thus, those precepts cannot be served. 12
And, again, sir, shall we sow the headland with wheat? 13

SHALLOW With red wheat, Davy. But for William
cook – are there no young pigeons?

DAVY Yes, sir. Here is now the smith's note for shoeing 16
and plow irons.

SHALLOW Let it be cast and paid. Sir John, you shall not 18
be excused.

DAVY Now, sir, a new link to the bucket must needs be 20
had. And, sir, do you mean to stop any of William's
wages, about the sack he lost the other day at Hinckley
fair?

SHALLOW A shall answer it. Some pigeons, Davy, a cou- 24
ple of short-legged hens, a joint of mutton, and any
pretty little tiny kickshaws, tell William cook. 26

DAVY Doth the man of war stay all night, sir?

SHALLOW Yea, Davy. I will use him well. A friend i' th' 28
court is better than a penny in purse. Use his men well,
Davy, for they are arrant knaves and will backbite. 30

DAVY No worse than they are backbitten, sir, for they 31
have marvelous foul linen.

SHALLOW Well conceited, Davy. About thy business, 33
Davy.

DAVY I beseech you, sir, to countenance William Visor 35
of Woncot against Clement Perkes o' th' hill. 36

SHALLOW There is many complaints, Davy, against that
Visor. That Visor is an arrant knave, on my knowledge.

DAVY I grant your worship that he is a knave, sir, but
yet, God forbid, sir, but a knave should have some 40

---

12 *precepts* warrants   13 *headland* unplowed strip between two plowed
fields   16 *smith's note* blacksmith's bill   18 *cast* added up   20 *link* chain or
handle   24 *answer* pay for   26 *kickshaws* delicacies (from the French
quelque choses)   28 *use* treat   31 *backbitten* i.e., by lice and fleas   33 *Well
conceited* very clever   35 *countenance* favor (in a judgment)   36 *Woncot,
Perkes* (Gloucestershire names)

countenance at his friend's request. An honest man, sir,
is able to speak for himself, when a knave is not. I have
served your worship truly, sir, this eight years, and if I
44 cannot once or twice in a quarter bear out a knave
against an honest man, I have but a very little credit
with your worship. The knave is mine honest friend,
sir. Therefore, I beseech you, let him be countenanced.

SHALLOW Go to, I say he shall have no wrong. Look
about, Davy. *[Exit Davy.]* Where are you, Sir John?
50 Come, come, come, off with your boots. Give me your
hand, Master Bardolph.

BARDOLPH I am glad to see your worship.

SHALLOW I thank thee with all my heart, kind Master
Bardolph. *[To the Page]* And welcome, my tall fellow.
Come, Sir John.

FALSTAFF I'll follow you, good Master Robert Shallow.
[Exit Shallow.] Bardolph, look to our horses. *[Exeunt*
58 *Bardolph and Page.]* If I were sawed into quantities, I
should make four dozen of such bearded hermits' staves
60 as Master Shallow. It is a wonderful thing to see the sem-
61 blable coherence of his men's spirits and his. They, by
observing him, do bear themselves like foolish justices;
63 he, by conversing with them, is turned into a justice-
like serving-man. Their spirits are so married in con-
65 junction with the participation of society that they
flock together in consent, like so many wild geese. If I
had a suit to Master Shallow, I would humor his men
68 with the imputation of being near their master. If to his
69 men, I would curry with Master Shallow that no man
70 could better command his servants. It is certain that ei-
71 ther wise bearing or ignorant carriage is caught, as men
take diseases, one of another. Therefore let men take

---

44 *bear out* support   58 *quantities* little pieces   60–61 *semblable coherence*
close correspondence   61 *his men's* i.e., his servants   63 *conversing* associat-
ing   65 *with . . . society* by close acquaintance   68 *with . . . near* by pretending to be friends with their master   69 *curry with* i.e., flatter   71
carriage behavior

heed of their company. I will devise matter enough out 73
of this Shallow to keep Prince Harry in continual
laughter the wearing out of six fashions, which is four 75
terms, or two actions, and a shall laugh without inter- 76
vallums. O, it is much that a lie with a slight oath and a
jest with a sad brow will do with a fellow that never had 78
the ache in his shoulders! O, you shall see him laugh till
his face be like a wet cloak ill laid up! 80

SHALLOW   *[Within]* Sir John!

FALSTAFF   I come, Master Shallow, I come, Master Shallow.

                                                    [Exit.]

                          *

∾ **V.2** *Enter Warwick, [meeting the] Lord Chief Justice.*

WARWICK
How now, my lord chief justice! whither away?

CHIEF JUSTICE
How doth the king?

WARWICK
Exceeding well. His cares are now all ended.

CHIEF JUSTICE
I hope, not dead.

WARWICK   He's walked the way of nature,
And to our purposes he lives no more.

CHIEF JUSTICE
I would his majesty had called me with him.
The service that I truly did his life   7
Hath left me open to all injuries.

---

73 *matter* i.e., for stories   75–76 *four terms* i.e., Michaelmas, Hilary, Easter,
and Trinity terms (the English names for the terms of the legal year)   76 *actions* lawsuits; *a* he   76–77 *intervallums* intervals between court sessions
78–79 *that . . . shoulders* i.e., that has never encountered trials in the world
(and is hence a dupe)   80 *ill laid up* carelessly stored so that it wrinkles
    V.2 The royal court   7 *truly did* faithfully executed during (among his re-
puted services was sending Prince Henry to prison for striking him)

WARWICK
  Indeed I think the young king loves you not.
CHIEF JUSTICE
10 I know he doth not, and do arm myself
  To welcome the condition of the time,
  Which cannot look more hideously upon me
  Than I have drawn it in my fantasy.
        Enter [Prince] John [of Lancaster], Thomas [of
        Clarence], and Humphrey [of Gloucester, with
        Westmoreland].
WARWICK
14 Here come the heavy issue of dead Harry.
  O that the living Harry had the temper
  Of him, the worst of these three gentlemen!
  How many nobles then should hold their places
18 That must strike sail to spirits of vile sort!
CHIEF JUSTICE
  O God, I fear all will be overturned!
LANCASTER
20 Good morrow, cousin Warwick, good morrow.
GLOUCESTER, CLARENCE
  Good morrow, cousin.
LANCASTER
22 We meet like men that had forgot to speak.
WARWICK
23 We do remember, but our argument
  Is all too heavy to admit much talk.
LANCASTER
  Well, peace be with him that hath made us heavy.
CHIEF JUSTICE
  Peace be with us, lest we be heavier.
GLOUCESTER
  O, good my lord, you have lost a friend indeed,

---

14 *heavy issue* grieving sons   18 *strike sail* make way for; salute   22 *forgot*
forgotten   23 *argument* subject

And I dare swear you borrow not that face
Of seeming sorrow, it is sure your own.
LANCASTER
Though no man be assured what grace to find,   30
You stand in coldest expectation.   31
I am the sorrier. Would 'twere otherwise.
CLARENCE
Well, you must now speak Sir John Falstaff fair,   33
Which swims against your stream of quality.   34
CHIEF JUSTICE
Sweet princes, what I did, I did in honor,
Led by the impartial conduct of my soul,
And never shall you see that I will beg
A ragged and forestalled remission.   38
If truth and upright innocency fail me,
I'll to the king my master that is dead,   40
And tell him who hath sent me after him.
WARWICK
Here comes the prince.
    Enter the Prince [as King Henry the Fifth] and Blunt.
CHIEF JUSTICE
Good morrow, and God save your majesty!
KING
This new and gorgeous garment, majesty,
Sits not so easy on me as you think.
Brothers, you mix your sadness with some fear.
This is the English, not the Turkish court.   47
Not Amurath an Amurath succeeds,
But Harry Harry. Yet be sad, good brothers,
For, by my faith, it very well becomes you.   50
Sorrow so royally in you appears

---

30 *grace to find* favor he will find (from Henry V)   31 *coldest* most un-
promising   33 *speak . . . fair* speak well of Sir John Falstaff   34 *swims . . .
quality* goes against the grain of your character   38 *ragged . . . remission* be-
grudged pardon   47 *Turkish court* (renowned for despotism, as in the act of
Amurath, who had his brothers strangled upon achieving the throne)

52   That I will deeply put the fashion on
      And wear it in my heart. Why then, be sad,
54   But entertain no more of it, good brothers,
      Than a joint burden laid upon us all.
56   For me, by heaven, I bid you be assured,
      I'll be your father and your brother too.
      Let me but bear your love, I'll bear your cares.
      Yet weep that Harry's dead, and so will I,
60   But Harry lives, that shall convert those tears
61   By number into hours of happiness.

PRINCES
      We hope no other from your majesty.

KING
63   You all look strangely on me.
          [To the Chief Justice]   And you most.
      You are, I think, assured I love you not.

CHIEF JUSTICE
65   I am assured, if I be measured rightly,
      Your majesty hath no just cause to hate me.

KING
      No?
      How might a prince of my great hopes forget
      So great indignities you laid upon me?
70   What! Rate, rebuke, and roughly send to prison
71   The immediate heir of England! Was this easy?
72   May this be washed in Lethe, and forgotten?

CHIEF JUSTICE
73   I then did use the person of your father.
74   The image of his power lay then in me.
      And, in the administration of his law,
      Whiles I was busy for the commonwealth,
      Your highness pleasèd to forget my place,

---

52 *deeply* solemnly   54 *entertain* consider, dwell upon   56 *For* as for   61
By number i.e., each tear will become an hour of happiness   63 *strangely* sus-
piciously   65 *measured rightly* judged correctly   70 *Rate* chide, scold   71
easy slight, insignificant   72 *Lethe* (the river in Hades whose waters rinsed
away memory)   73 *use the person* act on behalf of   74 *image* symbol

The majesty and power of law and justice,
The image of the king whom I presented,   79
And struck me in my very seat of judgment.   80
Whereon, as an offender to your father,   81
I gave bold way to my authority
And did commit you. If the deed were ill,   83
Be you contented, wearing now the garland,   84
To have a son set your decrees at nought,   85
To pluck down justice from your awful bench,   86
To trip the course of law and blunt the sword
That guards the peace and safety of your person,
Nay, more, to spurn at your most royal image
And mock your workings in a second body.   90
Question your royal thoughts, make the case yours.
Be now the father and propose a son,   92
Hear your own dignity so much profaned,
See your most dreadful laws so loosely slighted,
Behold yourself so by a son disdained,
And then imagine me taking your part
And in your power soft silencing your son.
After this cold considerance, sentence me,   98
And, as you are a king, speak in your state   99
What I have done that misbecame my place,   100
My person, or my liege's sovereignty.
KING
You are right, justice, and you weigh this well.
Therefore still bear the balance and the sword.   103
And I do wish your honors may increase,
Till you do live to see a son of mine
Offend you and obey you, as I did.
So shall I live to speak my father's words:
"Happy am I, that have a man so bold

---

79 *presented* represented   81 *as* as you were   83 *commit you* i.e., to prison
84 *garland* i.e., the crown   85 *set . . . nought* value your laws at nothing   86
awful awesome   90 *your . . . body* your functions in a deputy   92 *propose*
imagine (yourself the father of)   98 *cold considerance* calm consideration
99 *state* royal capacity   103 *balance* i.e., the scale, a symbol of justice

109   That dares do justice on my proper son,
110   And not less happy, having such a son
      That would deliver up his greatness so
      Into the hands of justice." You did commit me.
      For which, I do commit into your hand
      The unstained sword that you have used to bear,
115   With this remembrance, that you use the same
116   With the like bold, just, and impartial spirit
      As you have done 'gainst me. There is my hand.
      You shall be as a father to my youth.
119   My voice shall sound as you do prompt mine ear,
120   And I will stoop and humble my intents
      To your well-practiced wise directions.
      And, princes all, believe me, I beseech you,
123   My father is gone wild into his grave,
124   For in his tomb lie my affections,
      And with his spirit sadly I survive,
126   To mock the expectation of the world,
127   To frustrate prophecies and to raze out
      Rotten opinion, who hath writ me down
129   After my seeming. The tide of blood in me
130   Hath proudly flowed in vanity till now.
      Now doth it turn and ebb back to the sea,
132   Where it shall mingle with the state of floods
      And flow henceforth in formal majesty.
      Now call we our high court of parliament.
      And let us choose such limbs of noble counsel
      That the great body of our state may go
      In equal rank with the best-governed nation;
      That war, or peace, or both at once, may be
      As things acquainted and familiar to us,
140   In which you, father, shall have foremost hand.

---

109 *proper* own   **115** *remembrance* reminder   **116** *like* same   **119** *sound* speak   **120** *intents* intentions   **123–24** *my . . . affections* my wildness is buried with my father   **124** *affections* wild desires   **126** *expectation* i.e., of his wildness   **127** *raze* erase   **129** *seeming* pretense, outer appearance   **130** *vanity* folly   **132** *state* majesty

Our coronation done, we will accite,   141
As I before remembered, all our state.   142
And, God consigning to my good intents,   143
No prince nor peer shall have just cause to say,
God shorten Harry's happy life one day!   *Exeunt.*

*

∾ **V.3** *Enter Sir John [Falstaff], Shallow, Silence, Davy,*
Bardolph, Page.

SHALLOW   Nay, you shall see my orchard, where, in an
arbor, we will eat a last year's pippin of my own graf-   2
fing, with a dish of caraways, and so forth. Come,   3
cousin Silence. And then to bed.

FALSTAFF   'Fore God, you have here a goodly dwelling
and a rich.

SHALLOW   Barren, barren, barren. Beggars all, beggars
all, Sir John. Marry, good air. Spread, Davy, spread,   8
Davy. Well said, Davy.   9

FALSTAFF   This Davy serves you for good uses. He is your   10
serving-man and your husband.   11

SHALLOW   A good varlet, a good varlet, a very good var-   12
let, Sir John. By the mass, I have drunk too much sack
at supper. A good varlet. Now sit down, now sit down.
Come, cousin.

SILENCE   Ah, sirrah! quoth-a, we shall   16
[Sings.]
Do nothing but eat, and make good cheer,
And praise God for the merry year,
When flesh is cheap and females dear,   19
And lusty lads roam here and there   20

---

141 *accite* summon   142 *state* nobles   143 *consigning* agreeing
V.3 Within Shallow's orchard   2 *pippin* apple   2–3 *graffing* grafting
3 *caraways* caraway seeds   8 *Spread* i.e., the tablecloth and settings   9 *said*
done   11 *husband* steward, household manager   12 *varlet* servant   16
quoth-a said he   19 *flesh* meat

> So merrily,
> And ever among so merrily.

FALSTAFF There's a merry heart! Good Master Silence,
24 I'll give you a health for that anon.

SHALLOW Give Master Bardolph some wine, Davy.

DAVY Sweet sir, sit, I'll be with you anon. Most sweet sir,
27 sit. Master page, good master page, sit. Proface! What
28 you want in meat, we'll have in drink. But you must
29 bear, the heart's all.   *[Exit.]*

30 SHALLOW Be merry, Master Bardolph, and, my little soldier there, be merry.

SILENCE *[Sings.]*
> Be merry, be merry, my wife has all,
> For women are shrews, both short and tall.
> 'Tis merry in hall when beards wag all,
35 > And welcome merry Shrovetide.
> Be merry, be merry.

FALSTAFF I did not think Master Silence had been a man
of this mettle.

SILENCE Who, I? I have been merry twice and once ere
40 now.

Enter Davy.

41 DAVY *[To Bardolph]* There's a dish of leather-coats for
you.

SHALLOW Davy!

DAVY Your worship! *[To Bardolph]* I'll be with you
straight. – A cup of wine, sir?

SILENCE *[Sings.]*
> A cup of wine that's brisk and fine,
47 > And drink unto the leman mine,
> And a merry heart lives long-a.

FALSTAFF Well said, Master Silence.

---

24 *give you a* drink your; *anon* shortly   27 *Proface* (a welcome to dinner, meaning "May it do you good")   28 *want* lack; *meat* food   29 *bear* be patient   35 *Shrovetide* feast season prior to Lent   41 *leather-coats* russet apples   47 *leman* sweetheart

SILENCE   An we shall be merry, now comes in the sweet   *50*
o' the night.
FALSTAFF   Health and long life to you, Master Silence.
SILENCE   *[Sings.]*
    Fill the cup, and let it come,   *53*
    I'll pledge you a mile to the bottom.   *54*
SHALLOW   Honest Bardolph, welcome. If thou want'st
anything, and wilt not call, beshrew thy heart. *[To the*   *56*
Page] Welcome, my little tiny thief, and welcome in-
deed too. I'll drink to Master Bardolph, and to all the
cabileros about London.   *59*
DAVY   I hope to see London once ere I die.   *60*
BARDOLPH   An I might see you there, Davy –
SHALLOW   By the mass, you'll crack a quart together, ha!   *62*
Will you not, Master Bardolph?
BARDOLPH   Yea, sir, in a pottle-pot.   *64*
SHALLOW   By God's liggens, I thank thee. The knave will   *65*
stick by thee, I can assure thee that. A will not out, he is   *66*
true bred.
BARDOLPH   And I'll stick by him, sir.
  One knocks at door.
SHALLOW   Why, there spoke a king. Lack nothing. Be
merry. Look who's at door there, ho! Who knocks?   *70*
            [Exit Davy.]
FALSTAFF   *[To Silence, seeing him drinking]* Why, now you
have done me right.   *72*
SILENCE   *[Sings.]*
    Do me right,
    And dub me knight.
    Samingo.   *75*
Is't not so?
FALSTAFF   'Tis so.

---

53 *let it come* pass it around **54** *pledge you a mile* drink to you even if it were
a mile **56** *beshrew* the devil take **59** *cabileros* gallants, young blades **62**
crack drink **64** *pottle-pot* two-quart vessel **65** *By . . . liggens* (an unex-
plained oath) **66** *out* pass out **72** *done me right* drunk as much as I have
75 *Samingo* Sir Mingo, the hero of the song (*mingo* from the Latin, to piss)

SILENCE   Is't so? Why then, say an old man can do somewhat.
    [Enter Davy.]
80 DAVY   An't please your worship, there's one Pistol come
from the court with news.
FALSTAFF   From the court! Let him come in.
    Enter Pistol.
How now, Pistol!
PISTOL   Sir John, God save you!
FALSTAFF   What wind blew you hither, Pistol?
PISTOL   Not the ill wind which blows no man to good.
Sweet knight, thou art now one of the greatest men in
this realm.
89 SILENCE   By'r lady, I think a be, but goodman Puff of
90   Barson.
PISTOL   Puff!
92   Puff i' thy teeth, most recreant coward base!
Sir John, I am thy Pistol and thy friend,
And helter-skelter have I rode to thee,
And tidings do I bring and lucky joys
96   And golden times and happy news of price.
97 FALSTAFF   I pray thee now, deliver them like a man of
this world.
PISTOL
99   A foutra for the world and worldlings base!
100   I speak of Africa and golden joys.
FALSTAFF
101   O base Assyrian knight, what is thy news?
102   Let King Cophetua know the truth thereof.
SILENCE   *[Sings.]*
103   And Robin Hood, Scarlet, and John.

---

89 *but* except for; *goodman* yeoman   92 *recreant* worthless   96 *price* great
worth   97–98 *man . . . world* a regular person   99 *foutra* fuck (from
French)   101 *Assyrian* i.e., pagan, alien   102 *Cophetua* (in a ballad, a king
who married a beggar maid)   103 *And . . . John* a line from another song

PISTOL
   Shall dunghill curs confront the Helicons?   104
   And shall good news be baffled?   105
   Then, Pistol, lay thy head in Furies' lap.   106
SHALLOW Honest gentleman, I know not your breeding.
PISTOL Why then, lament therefore.   108
SHALLOW Give me pardon, sir. If, sir, you come with
   news from the court, I take it there's but two ways, ei- 110
   ther to utter them, or to conceal them. I am, sir, under
   the king, in some authority.
PISTOL
   Under which king, Besonian? Speak, or die.   113
SHALLOW
   Under King Harry.
PISTOL   Harry the Fourth? or Fifth?
SHALLOW
   Harry the Fourth.
PISTOL   A foutra for thine office!
   Sir John, thy tender lambkin now is king.
   Harry the Fifth's the man. I speak the truth.
   When Pistol lies, do this, and fig me, like   118
   The bragging Spaniard.
FALSTAFF
   What, is the old king dead?   120
PISTOL
   As nail in door. The things I speak are just.   121
FALSTAFF Away, Bardolph! Saddle my horse. Master
   Robert Shallow, choose what office thou wilt in the
   land, 'tis thine. Pistol, I will double-charge thee with 124
   dignities.

---

104 *Helicons* poets 105 *baffled* disgraced, flouted 106 *Furies* i.e., the Furies of hell 108 *therefore* on that account 113 *Besonian* ignoramus 118 *fig* insult by inserting the thumb between index and third fingers (a gesture associated with Spaniards) 121 *just* true 124 *double-charge* (a play on Pistol's name)

BARDOLPH
> O joyful day!
> I would not take a knighthood for my fortune.

PISTOL
> What! I do bring good news.

FALSTAFF Carry Master Silence to bed. Master Shallow,
130 my Lord Shallow – be what thou wilt, I am fortune's
steward – get on thy boots. We'll ride all night. O sweet
Pistol! Away, Bardolph! *[Exit Bardolph.]* Come, Pistol,
utter more to me, and withal devise something to do
thyself good. Boot, boot, Master Shallow. I know the
young king is sick for me. Let us take any man's horses;
the laws of England are at my commandment. Blessed
are they that have been my friends, and woe to my lord
chief justice!

PISTOL
> Let vultures vile seize on his lungs also!
140 "Where is the life that late I led?" say they.
> Why, here it is. Welcome these pleasant days!   *Exeunt.*

＊

～ **V.4** *Enter Beadle and three or four Officers [with
Hostess Quickly and Doll Tearsheet].*

HOSTESS No, thou arrant knave, I would to God that I
might die, that I might have thee hanged. Thou hast
drawn my shoulder out of joint.

BEADLE The constables have delivered her over to me,
5   and she shall have whipping-cheer enough, I warrant
6   her. There hath been a man or two lately killed about
her.

---

140 *Where . . . led* (a fragment of an old song)
   V.4 A London street   **5** *whipping-cheer* a whipping for supper; *warrant*
promise   **6** *about* (1) on her account, (2) in her presence

DOLL   Nut-hook, nut-hook, you lie. Come on, I'll tell   8
thee what, thou damned tripe-visaged rascal, an the   9
child I now go with do miscarry, thou wert better thou   10
hadst struck thy mother, thou paper-faced villain.   11

HOSTESS   O the Lord, that Sir John were come! He
would make this a bloody day to somebody. But I pray
God the fruit of her womb miscarry!

BEADLE   If it do, you shall have a dozen of cushions   15
again. You have but eleven now. Come, I charge you   16
both go with me, for the man is dead that you and Pistol beat amongst you.   18

DOLL   I'll tell you what, you thin man in a censer, I will   19
have you as soundly swinged for this – you blue-bottle   20
rogue, you filthy famished correctioner, if you be not
swinged, I'll forswear half-kirtles.   22

BEADLE   Come, come, you she knight-errant, come.   23

HOSTESS   O God, that right should thus overcome
might! Well, of sufferance comes ease.   25

DOLL   Come, you rogue, come, bring me to a justice.

HOSTESS   Ay, come, you starved bloodhound.

DOLL   Goodman death, goodman bones!

HOSTESS   Thou atomy, thou!   29

DOLL   Come, you thin thing, come, you rascal.   30

BEADLE   Very well.   *[Exeunt.]*

*

---

8 *Nut-hook* a hooked stick used to capture branches for nut harvesting
9 *tripe-visaged* flabby-faced   10 *child . . . miscarry* (pleading pregnancy was a
way to avoid the death penalty)   11 *paper-faced* pale   15 *cushions* (the Beadle
accuses her of padding her dress in order to appear pregnant)   16 *charge*
order   18 *amongst you* together   19 *thin . . . censer* embossed figure on an in-
cense burner   20 *swinged* beaten; *blue-bottle* (beadles wore blue coats)   22
half-kirtles skirts   23 *knight-errant* (with a pun on "night-errant": one who
sins – is errant – by night)   25 *sufferance* suffering   29 *atomy* skeleton
(anatomy)   30 *rascal* thin deer

∾ **V.5** *Enter [Grooms as] strewers of rushes.*

1 FIRST GROOM More rushes, more rushes.

SECOND GROOM The trumpets have sounded twice.

THIRD GROOM 'Twill be two o'clock ere they come from
4 the coronation. Dispatch, dispatch.   *[Exeunt.]*
    *Trumpets sound, and the King and his train pass over
    the stage. After them enter Falstaff, Shallow, Pistol,
    Bardolph, and the Boy [Page].*

FALSTAFF Stand here by me, Master Robert Shallow, I
6 will make the king do you grace. I will leer upon him as
7 a comes by, and do but mark the countenance that he
    will give me.

PISTOL God bless thy lungs, good knight.

10 FALSTAFF Come here, Pistol, stand behind me. O, if I had
11 had time to have made new liveries, I would have be-
    stowed the thousand pound I borrowed of you. But 'tis
13 no matter; this poor show doth better. This doth infer
    the zeal I had to see him.

SHALLOW It doth so.

FALSTAFF It shows my earnestness of affection –

SHALLOW It doth so.

FALSTAFF My devotion –

SHALLOW It doth, it doth, it doth.

20 FALSTAFF As it were, to ride day and night, and not to
21 deliberate, not to remember, not to have patience to
22 shift me –

SHALLOW It is best, certain.

FALSTAFF But to stand stained with travel, and sweating
    with desire to see him, thinking of nothing else, putting

---

V.5 Before Westminster Abbey 1 *rushes* reeds (used to strew floors, and here
a street) 4 *Dispatch* hurry 6 *grace* honor; *leer* glance sideways 7 *countenance* face, expression 11 *liveries* clothing that marked the owner as a member of a noble household's retinue 11–12 *bestowed* spent 13 *infer* suggest
21 *deliberate* calculate 22 *shift me* change my clothing

all affairs else in oblivion, as if there were nothing else to
be done but to see him.

PISTOL   'Tis "semper idem," for "absque hoc nihil est."   28
'Tis all in every part.

SHALLOW   'Tis so, indeed.   30

PISTOL
My knight, I will inflame thy noble liver,   31
And make thee rage.

Thy Doll, and Helen of thy noble thoughts,   33
Is in base durance and contagious prison,   34
Haled thither   35
By most mechanical and dirty hand.   36
Rouse up revenge from ebon den with fell Alecto's   37
snake.
For Doll is in. Pistol speaks nought but truth.

FALSTAFF
I will deliver her.

PISTOL
There roared the sea, and trumpet-clangor sounds.   40
[The trumpets sound.] Enter the King and his
train [, the Lord Chief Justice among them].

FALSTAFF
God save thy grace, King Hal, my royal Hal!

PISTOL
The heavens thee guard and keep, most royal imp of
fame!

FALSTAFF
God save thee, my sweet boy!

KING
My lord chief justice, speak to that vain man.   44

---

28 *semper idem* always the same; *absque . . . est* without this, nothing   **31**
liver (regarded as the seat of the passions)   **33** *Helen* i.e., of Troy, a legendary
beauty   **34** *durance* imprisonment   **35** *Haled* taken, hauled off   **36** *mechanical* workman's   **37** *ebon* black; *Alecto* one of the Furies (who had snakes
for hair)   **44** *vain* foolish

CHIEF JUSTICE
Have you your wits? Know you what 'tis you speak?

FALSTAFF
46 My king! My Jove! I speak to thee, my heart!

KING
I know thee not, old man. Fall to thy prayers.
How ill white hairs become a fool and jester!
I have long dreamed of such a kind of man,
50 So surfeit-swelled, so old, and so profane,
But, being awaked, I do despise my dream.
52 Make less thy body hence, and more thy grace.
53 Leave gormandizing. Know the grave doth gape
For thee thrice wider than for other men.
Reply not to me with a fool-born jest.
Presume not that I am the thing I was,
For God doth know, so shall the world perceive,
That I have turned away my former self.
So will I those that kept me company.
60 When thou dost hear I am as I have been,
Approach me, and thou shalt be as thou wast,
62 The tutor and the feeder of my riots.
Till then, I banish thee, on pain of death,
As I have done the rest of my misleaders,
65 Not to come near our person by ten mile.
66 For competence of life I will allow you,
That lack of means enforce you not to evils.
And, as we hear you do reform yourselves,
We will, according to your strengths and qualities,
70 Give you advancement. Be it your charge, my lord,
71 To see performed the tenor of our word.
Set on. *[Exeunt the King and his train.]*

FALSTAFF Master Shallow, I owe you a thousand pound.

---

46 *Jove* king of the classical gods **50** *surfeit-swelled* swollen from excessive eating **52** *make less* reduce; *hence* from now on **53** *gormandizing* eating to excess **62** *feeder* inciter **65** *our* my (he uses the royal plural) **66** *competence of life* a modest pension **71** *tenor* intention

SHALLOW   Yea, marry, Sir John, which I beseech you to
let me have home with me.

FALSTAFF   That can hardly be, Master Shallow. Do not
you grieve at this. I shall be sent for in private to him.
Look you, he must seem thus to the world. Fear not
your advancements; I will be the man yet that shall
make you great.   80

SHALLOW   I cannot well perceive how, unless you should
give me your doublet and stuff me out with straw. I beseech you, good Sir John, let me have five hundred of
my thousand.

FALSTAFF   Sir, I will be as good as my word. This that you
heard was but a color.   86

SHALLOW   A color that I fear you will die in, Sir John.   87

FALSTAFF   Fear no colors. Go with me to dinner. Come,   88
Lieutenant Pistol, come, Bardolph. I shall be sent for
soon at night.   90

    *Enter [the Lord Chief] Justice and Prince John [of
    Lancaster, with Officers].*

CHIEF JUSTICE

Go, carry Sir John Falstaff to the Fleet.   91
Take all his company along with him.

FALSTAFF

My lord, my lord —

CHIEF JUSTICE

I cannot now speak. I will hear you soon.
Take them away.

PISTOL

"Si fortuna me tormenta, spero contenta."   96
    Exeunt [all but Prince John and the Chief Justice].

LANCASTER

I like this fair proceeding of the king's.
He hath intent his wonted followers   98

---

86 *color* pretense **87** *color* (with pun on "collar," or hangman's noose) **88**
colors enemy **91** *Fleet* a London prison **96** *Si . . . contenta* (see note to
II.4.174) **98** *wonted* past, usual

Shall all be very well provided for,
100 But all are banished till their conversations
Appear more wise and modest to the world.
CHIEF JUSTICE
And so they are.
LANCASTER
The king hath called his parliament, my lord.
CHIEF JUSTICE
He hath.
LANCASTER
I will lay odds that, ere this year expire,
106 We bear our civil swords and native fire
As far as France. I heard a bird so sing,
Whose music, to my thinking, pleased the king.
Come, will you hence?   *[Exeunt.]*

*

∾ Epilogue

110

[Spoken by a Dancer]

First my fear, then my curtsy, last my speech. My fear is,
your displeasure; my curtsy, my duty; and my speech, to
beg your pardons. If you look for a good speech now, you
4 undo me, for what I have to say is of mine own making,
5 and what indeed I should say will, I doubt, prove mine own
6 marring. But to the purpose, and so to the venture. Be it
known to you, as it is very well, I was lately here in the end
8 of a displeasing play, to pray your patience for it and to
9 promise you a better. I meant indeed to pay you with this,
10 which, if like an ill venture it come unluckily home, I
11 break, and you, my gentle creditors, lose. Here I promised

---

106 *civil swords* used in civil wars
     Epilogue 4 *undo* ruin   5 *doubt* fear   6 *venture* matter at hand   8 *play*
(unidentified)   9 *this* i.e., this play   10 *ill venture* unfortunate trading voy-
age   11 *break* (1) i.e., my promise, (2) go bankrupt

you I would be and here I commit my body to your mercies. Bate me some and I will pay you some and, as most 13
debtors do, promise you infinitely.

If my tongue cannot entreat you to acquit me, will
you command me to use my legs? And yet that were but
light payment, to dance out of your debt. But a good conscience will make any possible satisfaction, and so would
I. All the gentlewomen here have forgiven me. If the gentlemen will not, then the gentlemen do not agree with the 20
gentlewomen, which was never seen before in such an assembly.

One word more, I beseech you. If you be not too
much cloyed with fat meat, our humble author will continue 24
the story, with Sir John in it, and make you merry
with fair Katherine of France. Where, for anything I
know, Falstaff shall die of a sweat, unless already a be
killed with your hard opinions, for Oldcastle died a martyr 28
, and this is not the man. My tongue is weary. When
my legs are too, I will bid you good night, and so kneel 30
down before you, but, indeed, to pray for the queen.

---

13 *Bate me* relieve me of some of my debts   **24–25** *continue* i.e., in *Henry V*
28 *Oldcastle* (Falstaff was originally called Oldcastle, until Shakespeare was
required by a descendant to change the name; Oldcastle was executed in
1417 for treason, and later celebrated, in Shakespeare's time, as a martyr for
Protestantism)

FOR THE BEST IN PAPERBACKS, LOOK FOR THE 🐧

The distinguished Pelican Shakespeare series, newly revised
to be the premier choice for students, professors, and
general readers well into the 21st century

NOW AVAILABLE

Antony and Cleopatra
ISBN 0-14-071452-9

Much Ado About Nothing
ISBN 0-14-71480-4

The Comedy of Errors
ISBN 0-14-071474-X

The Narrative Poems
ISBN 0-14-071481-2

Coriolanus
ISBN 0-14-071473-1

Richard III
ISBN 0-14-071483-9

Cymbeline
ISBN 0-14-071472-3

Romeo and Juliet
ISBN 0-14-071484-7

Henry IV, Part I
ISBN 0-14-071456-1

The Tempest
ISBN 0-14-071485-5

Henry IV, Part 2
ISBN 0-14-071457-X

Timon of Athens
ISBN 0-14-071487-1

Henry V
ISBN 0-14-071458-8

Titus Andronicus
ISBN 0-14-071491-X

King Lear
ISBN 0-14-071476-6

Twelfth Night
ISBN 0-14-071489-8

King Lear
(The Quarto and Folio Texts)
ISBN 0-14-071490-1

The Two Gentlemen of Verona
ISBN 0-14-071461-8

The Winter's Tale
ISBN 0-14-071488-X

Macbeth
ISBN 0-14-071478-2

FORTHCOMING

FOR THE BEST IN PAPERBACKS, LOOK FOR THE 🐧

In every corner of the world, on every subject under the sun, Penguin represents quality and variety—the very best in publishing today.

For complete information about books available from Penguin—including Penguin Classics, Penguin Compass, and Puffins—and how to order them, write to us at the appropriate address below. Please note that for copyright reasons the selection of books varies from country to country.

In the United States: Please write to *Penguin Group (USA), P.O. Box 12289 Dept. B, Newark, New Jersey 07101-5289* or call 1-800-788-6262.

In the United Kingdom: Please write to *Dept. EP, Penguin Books Ltd, Bath Road, Harmondsworth, West Drayton, Middlesex UB7 0DA.*

In Canada: Please write to *Penguin Books Canada Ltd, 90 Eglinton Avenue East, Suite 700, Toronto, Ontario M4P 2Y3.*

In Australia: Please write to *Penguin Books Australia Ltd, P.O. Box 257, Ringwood, Victoria 3134.*

In New Zealand: Please write to *Penguin Books (NZ) Ltd, Private Bag 102902, North Shore Mail Centre, Auckland 10.*

In India: Please write to *Penguin Books India Pvt Ltd, 11 Panchsheel Shopping Centre, Panchsheel Park, New Delhi 110 017.*

In the Netherlands: Please write to *Penguin Books Netherlands bv, Postbus 3507, NL-1001 AH Amsterdam.*

In Germany: Please write to *Penguin Books Deutschland GmbH, Metzlerstrasse 26, 60594 Frankfurt am Main.*

In Spain: Please write to *Penguin Books S. A., Bravo Murillo 19, 1° B, 28015 Madrid.*

In Italy: Please write to *Penguin Italia s.r.l., Via Benedetto Croce 2, 20094 Corsico, Milano.*

In France: Please write to *Penguin France, Le Carré Wilson, 62 rue Benjamin Baillaud, 31500 Toulouse.*

In Japan: Please write to *Penguin Books Japan Ltd, Kaneko Building, 2-3-25 Koraku, Bunkyo-Ku, Tokyo 112.*

In South Africa: Please write to *Penguin Books South Africa (Pty) Ltd, Private Bag X14, Parkview, 2122 Johannesburg.*